Praise for *Blue Bias:*
An Ex-Cop Turned Philosopher Examines the Learning and Resolve Necessary to End Hidden Prejudice in Policing

"An authoritative, and blessedly non-authoritarian, book on policing in America."

—NORM STAMPER, Seattle Chief of Police (Ret.),
author of *Breaking Rank* and *To Protect and Serve*

"Charles Hayes' goal as an ex-cop is to teach the science underlying implicit bias... He succeeds admirably at this. This is an important book."

—ROBERT M. SAPOLSKY, author of *Behave* and *Why Zebras Don't Get Ulcers*

"Charles Hayes assembles the latest research from brain science and psychology to help protect lives."

—R. DOUGLAS FIELDS, PHD, author of *Why We Snap:*
Understanding the Rage Circuit in Your Brain

"An eye-opening glimpse into what (good) police work entails."

—MIHALY CSIKSZENTMIHALYI, author of *Flow* and *The Evolving Self*

"What Hayes writes here contributes highly to the loftiest (and necessary) goal of American policing."

—DAVID COUPER, Madison Chief of Police (Ret.), author of
Arrested Development and *Telling It Like It Is*

"*Blue Bias* offers a ground-breaking and revolutionary formula for curtailing bias, prejudice, excessive force, and so forth within the arena of law enforcement. Essential reading."

—JOHN F. SCHUMAKER, author of *Wings of Illusion* and *The Age of Insanity*

Evolving in a
DANGEROUS
World Made
RACISM
INEVITABLE

Concerned Citizens, Police Officers,
and Teachers Can Help Change This

BY CHARLES D. HAYES

AUTODIDACTIC PRESS

WASILLA, ALASKA

Autodidactic Press
P. O. Box 872749
Wasilla, AK 99687
www.autodidactic.com

First Edition

ISBN-13: 978-0-9885795-2-1, ISBN-10: 0-988579529 (softcover)
ISBN-13: 978-0-9885795-1-4, ISBN-10: 0-9885795-1-0 (eBook)

Library of Congress Control Number: 2022911183

Book design: Shannon Bodie, BookWiseDesign.com

Names: Hayes, Charles D. (Charles Douglas), author.

Title: Evolving in a dangerous world made racism inevitable : concerned citizens,
    police officers, and teachers can help change this / by Charles D. Hayes.

Description: First edition. | Wasilla, Alaska : Autodidactic Press, [2022] | Includes
    bibliographical references and index.

Identifiers: ISBN: 978-0-9885795-2-1 | LCCN: 2022911183

Subjects: LCSH: United States--Race relations. | Culture conflict--United
    States. | Social conflict--United States--Psychological aspects. |
    Prejudices--United States--Psychological aspects. | Racism--United
    States--Psychological aspects. | Race discrimination--United States--
    Psychological aspects. | Gender identity--Political aspects--United
    States. | Censorship--Political aspects--United States. | Race--Study
    and teaching--Political aspects--United States. | Sex differences--Study
    and teaching--Political aspects--United States. | Political psychology--
    United States. | Psychophysiology--United States.

Classification: LCC: E185.615 .H39 2022 | DDC: 305.800973--dc23

CONTENTS

INTRODUCTION

By the time this book is published, I will be 79 years old and less than a year from having had triple-bypass open-heart surgery. Such life events are stressful, but they are nothing compared to the emotional dread many of my generation feel because of the political danger we find ourselves in today. We are teetering on the brink of trading democracy for autocracy. This is being driven in part by politicians who weaponize our human differences using our tribalistic tendencies. The subject of race is used as a means of strategic polarization—when insecurities about identity are used to fog reasoning, millions of people will feel racial animus, instead of opting for the ideals of the better argument, which is crucial for the existence of democracy. We are facing nothing culturally that warrants the demonization of individuals, groups, or races of people. There are no valid reasons for tribalistic hatred in America. None.

Caveat: Having been interested in the subject of bias for more than a half century and after spending much of the past decade studying the subject intently, I can say with confidence that if you

1

are not the kind of person who can be persuaded by the better argument, then this book will be a waste of your time. Go to any work on Amazon about mitigating racial bias and read the reviews. You will likely find many examples of people dismissing antiracist works based purely on political grounds, rather than engaging with the writer's actual arguments. This mindset is emblematic of the difficulty in addressing an egregious social problem that, for every few steps forward, we take one or two back. But if you are amenable to the better argument, I believe you will find the evidence offered in this work is worthy of a paradigm shift about the subject of implicit bias, a stunning revelation when put into perspective given how long we have been arguing about race relations while making very little progress. An important caveat here is psychologist Gordon W. Allport's observation that, "Defeated intellectually, prejudice lingers emotionally."[1]

Addressing the problem of racial prejudice by explaining the way our minds work is often called behavioral realism, or biological realism. Some advocates for racial justice fear that, by biologizing racism, the history of explicit racism will be ignored or disregarded.[2] This may in some cases be a valid concern, but I see it as a separate issue. In *Race on the Brain: What Implicit Bias Gets Wrong About the Struggle for Racial Justice*, law professor Jonathan Kahn reminds us that implicit bias is not an end-all in and of itself, and he is right.[3] But we are talking about realism, so let's keep it real.

Trying to solve the problems of racial prejudice without dealing with how our minds default to subconscious assumptions is like trying to explain the subject of shadows without acknowledging the role of the sun. Indeed, the dynamics of implicit bias are not an end-all, but understanding the functioning of our subconscious provides the ammunition necessary to understand why racism is so hard to eradicate. Kahn suggests that neuroscience studies can have the effect of marginalizing the role of explicit biases, and while I agree this is possible, it is by no means inevitable.[4] Kahn's concerns about how we use what we have learned about implicit biases are warranted, however, and the potential for that to go wrong is made worse by current efforts to politicize race.

Defeating the inevitable backlash movements that follow positive measures for achieving racial justice requires a liberal arts effort of epic proportions against all the social components of tribalistic hatred, with every conceivable tool that can be put to work. I am all for this in every way possible. I don't personally know how to cancel tribalistic hatred. My goal is simply to help people, like me and my generation, who have unwittingly internalized cultural biases, but who care deeply about wanting to stop them from unintentionally resurfacing and resulting in acts that mimic explicit bias.

Kahn is right that implicit bias cannot be understood apart from its social and historical context.[5] Historical context provides the impetus for default behaviors caused precisely because of encountering cultural differences with *others*.[6] The sun causes shadows; likewise, putting an emphasis on differences when we assume people are outsiders will result in the internalization of biases. In a historical context, expressed social differences are inevitable, conflict is inevitable, and a case could be made that war and genocide cannot be ruled out. Kahn argues that behavioral realism has a lot to offer (but it is no magic bullet), and that raising awareness is a good thing.[7] Understanding implicit bias doesn't solve the problem of systemic bias and age-old racial hatred, but surely it opens a door that must be opened.

The incessant academic and politically contrived arguments about the exact nature of racism keep us from acting on what we know. Kahn says, "Racism is protean: as you try to grasp it, it changes form."[8] I agree wholeheartedly. Think about it this way: Given the anatomical functioning of human gray matter in the context of widespread social relations among peoples of the world, with dramatically different customs and traditions, is there any way under the sun to have avoided racial biases, given the way we react tribally to our differences? I don't think so.

Kahn points out that juries and prosecutors continue to believe it is reasonable for police officers to fear Black men. If we give credence to behavioral realism, then it can be argued that such fear is justified.[9] But as I will point out in myriad ways, fear may be too strong a term. Our limbic system notes our tribalistic differences in matters of degree in the blink of an eye and it doesn't take much of a difference for us to make decidedly different judgments. Moreover, if this biological process is involved in cases where caution or fear seem to be the culprit, then how in heaven's name do we solve this problem without taking our biology into account? What is at stake is far more important than whose academic argument prevails.

Sometimes, the things in life that are most apparent are very hard to see simply because they are so obvious. We split the atom, put man on the moon and decoded DNA, yet the manifestly evident conflict between our consciousness and unconsciousness remains elusive, obscure, and for all practical purposes, ignored by people who should know better. Nearly seven decades ago, Gordon W. Allport, in discussing bigotry, noticed a sharp cleavage between consciousness and the subconscious.[10] In my view, this distance is part of the reason we are so reluctant to examine sensitive subjects deeply. Why is common sense about bias so uncommon? When one considers the tribalistic history of *Homo sapiens* and the dangers our species has commonly encountered for thousands of generations, the ambiguity of the subject of human bias as an intuitive predilection to be wary of danger should instantaneously make sense.

Yet why do so many people consider Critical Race Theory, for example, so threatening? A sincere level of interest in racial bias should have put this subject in clear perspective at least a half century ago. Critical Race Theory is a *graduate-school-level* effort to deconstruct systemic racism in the law. It is not being taught in public schools. Neither is the history being taught in public schools in any way in the vicinity of what truly occurred regarding race. Harry Truman said, "The only thing new in the world is the history you don't know."[11] How unfortunate that this lack of knowledge can also be used to manipulate people based solely on fear. How do we know where we are, if we don't know where we have been? If we don't know where we have been, we can't know who we are now or where we might go.

The story of racism in America is as horrific as the darkest periods of world history, and the reasons for not wanting to admit this to schoolchildren are easy to understand. However, to *not* admit that this appalling travesty occurred is to set us up to repeat the mistakes of the past and to continue perpetuating systemic racism in the present. Explicit bias, that old-fashioned hatred for hatred's sake, is very much alive in America today. There are more than a thousand active hate groups in the country and hate crimes have been on the rise for a decade.[12] This social malady calls for a change in perspectives.

In *Hatred: Understanding Our Most Dangerous Emotion*, Berit Brogaard writes:

> **To be sure, systematic racism is not simply the sum total of people's explicit and implicit racial prejudices. Rather, it is first and foremost constituted by existing**

norms, laws, and regulations that breed social injustice. However, systemic racism persists in our society because it's tolerated by those of us who benefit from its existence.[13]

Brogaard doesn't, however, take a very deep dive into the unvarnished history of race in America, nor does she explore the sacrifices and hardships endured by slaves in the South and their descendants. What they have suffered and achieved should eradicate any and all excuses for hatred on the basis of race.

Explicit bias is often a part of tradition, learned animosity passed from one generation to the next as what has been commonly accepted as conventional wisdom. Implicit biases, however, are simply stereotypic cultural assumptions we have internalized as representing reality, invariably without realizing we have done so. This disconnect exists, as we will see, because our subconscious and our conscious selves are out of sync. My objective in this work is to focus on the persistent prevalence of implicit bias.

Explicit bias is easier to address, because a change of mind can successfully mitigate it, but the great difficulty in alleviating implicit bias is convincing people that it exists, and there are clear historical consequences. But the old traditional hatred is present today to such a degree that it makes the case for addressing implicit bias harder—much harder—because people who don't consciously have negative views against minorities don't want to be associated with racism in any way, which is understandable.

Liberal and conservative politics aside, implicit biases exist beneath our conscious awareness. If we have grown up in a culture where systemic racism is pervasive, then our personal opinions about whether we hold racist views are pretty much worthless. Our subconscious selves are not concerned with things as they should be, only things as they appear, and if the people we grow up with share a common belief, we are likely to be influenced by their views, whether we agree with their collective assessments or not. As we will see, it takes more than being against racism to mitigate implicit biases.

I will address the subject of implicit bias primarily in the context of policing, because this is an area that I have some experience and an intense interest in. However, teachers are the explainers in our society, so I will address them as well. Make no mistake: This is a subject that applies to every aspect of global society. Concerned citizens willing to take up the mantle of eliminating implicit bias already have the most important qualification, which is passion. Policing is an area where accusations about racial bias routinely make headlines. Incidents that remind us of George Floyd occur far too often. Sometimes they happen because of explicit racism, but often, events that result in the appearance of racial prejudice occur without malice aforethought, simply because of how human brains work. Unfortunately, this is not common knowledge. Schoolteachers are at the forefront in arming us with the common knowledge necessary to make our society socially viable. Explaining how evolution wired humanity for tribal wariness is something vital that is missing in public education.

In the 1960s, after serving a four-year hitch in the Marines, I joined the Dallas Police Department. I began the job with over-the-top enthusiasm. At first it was fun. I looked forward to going to work every day. It took several months to get the hang of what was going on. Many times during training, my senior partner would turn on the red lights to stop a car and I wouldn't know why because I hadn't seen the violation that he did. But after a while, everything clicked, and I started seeing violations and potential crimes in progress everywhere. The first couple of years went by fast. Gradually, my enthusiasm began to wane, and after another year or so, I began to get increasingly angry when answering disturbance calls because they seemed so infantile. I began to resent being called to handle situations that I deemed childish and unnecessary. After four years, I left the department, filled with existential disgust at having been unprepared psychologically to deal with so much aberrant behavior.

When I wrote *Blue Bias*, I made it clear that politically, I identify as liberal. But to take the view that policing is political is to miss the whole point of the civic and moral aspiration to protect and serve. There should be nothing inherently political in law enforcement—justice is supposed to be blind. The key examples of bias (race, age, gender, appearance, and class), with regard to policing, are not in essence political; they are instead critical components of human decency. In each case, everyone, not just police officers, needs to fully understand that our gut-level tendencies to judge other people are a part of our evolutionary makeup. We must fully understand this to compensate for the fact that we no longer live in the Stone Age. We need to be made thoroughly aware of how our minds work, not just to keep us safe, but to keep us from distancing ourselves from our fellow citizens because of minor differences.

We know from experience that venturing too far left or right politically results in disaster. A balance of our left and right political predilections is necessary to our continued success as a Republic. But where we are today is that the effects of social media are enabling a retribalization through self-selection and ideological amplification. Today the extreme polarization in America has both the political left and right often becoming so enraged by the actions of the opposition as to metaphorically relegate them to the insular cortex, which is the headquarters of disgust. Thus it is game-over in negotiating common ground or compromise because each group perceives the other as being unworthy of consideration. It is difficult to overstate the seriousness of polarization at the level of disgust. Neuroscientist Robert M. Sapolsky put it this way: "When people's insulae activates at the thought of Thems, you can check one thing off your genocide list."[14] This book is an effort to dial this back.

When I consider the public awareness of racial bias today— for example, George Floyd's death at the hands of police officers in Minnesota in 2020—my memories of Dallas in the 1960s seem like they occurred on another planet. In those days, Dallas was still enduring widespread denunciation because of the assassination of President John F. Kennedy. But when I compare the public attitudes about racism, both implicit and explicit, it is clear to me that explicit racism then was closer to the rule, rather than the exception. Implicit bias in those days inevitably became grounds for explicit bias. We have made progress in the public's understanding of racial bias, but for all that has been learned in biology and neuroscience, we are still not even close to making what has been discovered about bias public knowledge to such a degree that it can have a positive effect on public behavior.

A few years after I gave up policing, I became insatiably interested in the behavioral sciences and I began to regret having left law enforcement. Through intensive self-education, I had at last developed the perspective necessary to handle the angst that comes with the job, but I was then employed by Arco on Alaska's North Slope, and I worked a week on/week off shift. I began to use my off time to read intensely and to write books and essays about the value of self-education. I have reflected for over a half century on my policing experience, and I have spent almost seven years now studying pro and con police literature, together with learning how biology and neuroscience affect police behavior, which is critical to improving policing in America.

But policing is only one theme of this book. The subject of racial bias is everybody's business. America's future depends on Americans understanding how our brains have evolved with an innate obsession for categorizing and stereotyping—an evolutionary process over which we have no control. Fair warning, some of the repetition in this work is likely to be annoying, and the need to include it bothers me, but the unconscious biases that we all have internalized are themselves the result of incessant repetition. Being reminded only once or twice to address ideas that we are not familiar with simply won't cut it. We are all taught that stereotyping is wrong, so it is easy to understand how most of us are inclined to push back when we are accused of it, but as you will see, this process is something our brains evolved to do automatically.

My hope is to help mitigate racial bias by enlisting people on the front lines of socialization—concerned citizens, police officers, and teachers—to help spread the word about how our Stone Age biological predilections, if not addressed intellectually, work to our disadvantage, and that we desperately need to address racial relations in this country for our country's sake.

THE CULTURE WAR

In August of 2019, *The New York Times Magazine* published a piece by Nikole Hannah-Jones titled, "The 1619 Project," which pointed out the largely unacknowledged historical fact that a ship arrived in America with slaves in 1619 and, because of this, she argued, 1619 should be considered America's birth year. A political backlash ensued, resulting in the very subject of race becoming a lightning rod of controversy. In November of 2021, *The New York Times Magazine* published *The 1619 Project: A New Beginning* in book form. We are now experiencing a race-based cultural war in this country. The most valuable things we have learned so far may be lost if we allow the subject of race to stay weaponized.

Insightful books like *White Fragility: Why It's So Hard for White People to Talk About Racism* by Robin DiAngelo and *How to Be an Antiracist* by Ibram X. Kendi that call our attention to systemic racial biases are being attacked as if their intended objective is not to eliminate racial bias, but to divide America politically based on race. The issue of race is so thoroughly embedded in our

11

cultural traditions that it wouldn't be that much of a stretch for an alien visitor to suspect that the viral ingredients for racial discrimination might be in the water we drink.

I keep reading comments from people who decry so much emphasis about race in America, especially from those who still vehemently believe that their conscious minds have a slam-dunk grip on reality—that what they see is what they believe. They have it exactly backwards: What they believe is what they see. In her book, *White Fragility,* Robin DiAngelo has struck a nerve with such intensity that some people cannot or will not read her book. Not because it is not true, but, in my opinion, because they don't want it to be true. What I find truly frustrating is that there are so many people who accuse authors who focus on the ubiquity of racism of being guilty of calling too much attention to the subject. Those people simply haven't experienced oppression all of their lives because of racism and can have a difficult time comprehending how important the issue is for people who have.

An ideological backlash to antiracism is smoldering, and books are being published that claim the Black Lives Matter Movement has become a religion of the extreme left and has a plan to divide the country. Idealogues are characterizing this as a war against wokeness. If being woke is a pejorative status, then so is being *enlightened.* The term "woke" originated with Black intellectuals simply to describe people who fully comprehend the dynamics of racism, and because of this, "woke" conveys an aspirational affirmation: caring enough to understand what desperately needs to be understood for the sake of humanity's common cause.[15]

In *Woke, Inc: Inside Corporate America's Social Justice Scam,* entrepreneur Vivek Ramaswamy claims wokeness is "actually a religion" and he can prove it.[16] Ramaswamy was born in America, but his parents are from India, and they were born into India's caste system as Brahmins, the highest level of that system. He now says there is nothing to the caste system, that the notion of Brahmins being superior is untrue, but after reading his book, I don't think for a minute that he really believes it.[17] Ramaswamy says he is fed up with efforts to achieve a sense of moral fairness in corporations. He views himself as a capitalist in the true unencumbered sense of the term. He claims he can legally show that wokeness is a religion—and he has a law degree from Yale.[18] Now, I am not a lawyer, and I don't doubt that in some ways efforts to bring racial justice to corporate America may be flawed, but for someone who should be aware of how caste systems subjugate and oppress to be so insensitive as to dismiss their angst as a religion, while he is himself an admitted, fervent, true-believing capitalist, is steeped in irony. The deepest bedrock expression of spiritual devotion in all creeds is that their zeal, reflected in hardcore capitalists, qualifies them as representing the epitome of True Believers. Reverence, worship, and adulation are properties of religion—an obsessive concern to right racial injustices is not.

To me, Ramaswamy's hypocrisy is as jarring as fingernails scratching a blackboard. Pure capitalism without regard to the damage that business as usual is doing to the planet amounts to an unobstructed reign of environmental malignancy, yet he sees efforts to address climate change through corporate management as a political scam, which he also repeatedly links with concerns about gender equality and racism.[19] The way I read Ramaswamy, he believes that the only legit politics in business are his.

I support the Black Lives Matter Movement because I am sufficiently versed in the history of race, and particularly with the blemished history of policing that I have personally taken part in. The Black Lives Matter Movement, in my view, is simply a plea to pay attention to the statistically overwhelming reality of systemic racism in this country. Waging an ideological war against Critical Race Theory will only make matters worse, as everyone involved will simply double down and become more entrenched in their own rationales of confirmation bias. No one has a lock on virtue regarding theories about race—critical race theorists can also get things wrong—and the best example of this may be when it comes to forcing people to attend bias training who are against it. There are no known sure-fire ways to address the ubiquity of implicit racial bias in American culture, but there is a profound lesson to be observed. The number one criterion for mitigating racial bias is people who care deeply about doing so. This existential reality can't be over-emphasized. Forcing people to attend bias training who are adamantly against it because they don't clearly understand the reasons for the training is worse than just a futile effort. This practice can also up the angst of those oppressed by racial bias because it offers the illusion that fairness has thus been achieved.[20]

Caring is critical: People must be convinced that, because, of the way our brains process experience and a lifetime of socialization in a culture in which both implicit and explicit bias are present, it is very nearly impossible not to have internalized enough of the negative culture to show up statistically when we offer judgments regarding issues of race. Ironically, the full-blown atrocities that an in-depth study of policing in America regarding race reveals are likely only to persuade the persuadable that racial bias in law enforcement is indeed systemic.

We are a tribalistic species. We are so predisposed to absorb our life experience and fit in that we grow up talking like those whom we are raised with. We develop accents, which also become a basis for bias, in that other people will judge us based on nothing but how we sound to them when we speak. When we begin to comprehend our behavioral predilections based simply on how our minds process our experience, it should become immediately clear how futile and unproductive it is to demonize one another by playing the tiresome and endless badminton game of "You are a racist," "No, I am not."

In Steven Pinker's much-needed book, *Rationality: What It Is, Why It Seems Scarce, Why It Matters,* Pinker opines about how the murder of George Floyd led to "the adoption of a radical academic doctrine."[21] But I don't consider deconstructing the historical legality of systemic racial bias in law to be a radical idea. I think what is radical is refusing to face the historical reality of racism in America. Our history textbooks in public education have never been up to the task of making it crystal clear just how horrid and egregiously difficult life has been for minorities in this country, especially African Americans, Native Americans, and Latinos. This is a key impediment in arousing public sentiment to take the subject of racial bias seriously enough to successfully address the issue. Those who have no appreciation of the history of racism tend to substitute arrogance and animus for the knowledge necessary to deal with it.

Anyone who has not intently studied the period of 1860 through 1880 in America's history is simply unprepared to realize the full measure of the genealogy of racial hatred in this country, a schism so deep that the gap still divides ideological factions today. In 1865, the prospect that poor southern whites would be required to compete in a labor market with freed slaves evoked a bottomless soul-sick animus of resentment and incendiary rage with so much vitriolic malevolence the residue of this sentiment is still alive today in many parts of the South. For the freed slaves on the receiving end of this diabolical hatred, this viciousness was of a sufficient caliber that the feelings of cultural contempt it routinely implied were passed from one generation to the next, without need of a discussion to deliver the message. It's as if the fire has burned out, but there are still plenty of hot coals.[22]

Political scientist Charles Murray is the author of *Losing Ground* and *The Bell Curve*. He and I are the same age, but we seem to be living on different planets. For decades, Murray has tiptoed around the notion of inherent racial superiority. Sometimes he will spend an enormous number of words trying to cover up the simple notion that he assumes that white people are inherently a superior race. Murray is a bedrock believer in white supremacy, and he has a new book out titled *Facing Reality: Two Truths About Race in America* that should remove all doubt, had there been any. Murray himself has never faced the reality of what years of vengeful oppression have done to African American culture. He has been trying for decades to blame economic inequality on genetics.[23] A cursory examination of the success of Black men and women during and since Reconstruction should have nuked that idea a century ago.

Reconstruction history narrated by white Southern authors has tended to blame its failure entirely on African Americans, but the efforts of Black men and women during this period, though brief and purposely stymied with severe tactics, showed proof of the competence of Black citizens given a chance. W. E. B. Du Bois made that clear in *Black Reconstruction in America: 1860-1880*. Du Bois wrote:

It must be remembered and never forgotten that the civil war in the South which overthrew Reconstruction was a determined effort to reduce black labor as nearly as possible to a condition of unlimited exploitation and build a new class of capitalists on this foundation.[24]

About his claims of fairness, Du Bois said:

> I cannot believe that any unbiased mind, with an ideal
> of truth and of scientific judgment, can read the plain,
> authentic facts of our history, during 1860-1880, and
> come to conclusions essentially different from mine;
> and yet I stand virtually alone in this interpretation.[25]

In *Slavery by Another Name: The Re-Enslavement of Black Americans from the Civil War to World War II*, Douglas A. Blackmon shows how, after Emancipation, thousands of Black men in the South were subjected to trumped-up criminal charges by local sheriffs, solely for the purpose of being sentenced to prison so their labor could be leased to farmers, mine owners, or railroads. These prisoners numbered more than a hundred thousand, possibly twice that many, as there were hundreds of labor camps all over the South.[26]

In *Lynching in the New South: Georgia and Virginia, 1880-1930*, W. Fitzhugh Brundage describes a reign of terror in the South, horrific beyond any standards of human decency—events that to this day have escaped America's public-school textbooks coast to coast. Brundage tells us lynching was a southern obsession so common that Mark Twain sarcastically renamed the country the "United States of Lyncherdom."[27] Brundage reports that post-Reconstruction planters shot and killed thousands of Black people for arguing over labor contracts.[28] He quotes a Methodist minister who, in 1893, said the killing of Blacks is not "so an extraordinary occurrence that it needs explanation."[29] Black men were killed for "wild talk" like demanding higher wages.[30] What were referred to as "grave insults" led to lynchings.[31] I have barely touched the surface here on the unspeakable crimes against Black men and women that were readily accepted as southern justice.

Black people in America were denied equal education

opportunities for generations, and denied loans for homes, farms, and businesses, while subject to both legal and illegal red lining for a century. Consequently, what we have gotten are impoverished communities with people subjected to a double standard in policing which continues today. Then opponents use the diminished educational abilities of people living under such circumstances as evidence that they were inferior to begin with. The environment human beings grow up in is analogous to vegetable gardens. We don't berate vegetables that grow up in deficient soil by shouting at them to just shape up and grow, yet this is exactly what we do with minorities whose oppression in myriad ways perfectly explains why they are poor to begin with. This is Charles Murray in a nutshell. The groundswell of explicit racism during the past decade means Murray doesn't have to pretend anymore. He is talking IQ again.[32] The controversy that arose with the publication of *The Bell Curve* rendered Murray a little less adamant about his claims of racial superiority, but it is evident that he finds the current political climate friendly enough to get back in the game, so to speak, with what I deem is his bone-marrow-deep belief in white superiority.

Then there is *Woke Racism: How a New Religion Has Betrayed Black People in America* by linguist John McWhorter.[33] McWhorter's book is a high five for people who deny the existence of systemic racism. Those who laud it as being a great work will use it as evidence that the dust-up about racism is just as they thought—a big to-do about nothing. Rather than acknowledging that systemic racism exists, they will double down on it being a ruse. McWhorter offers little in this work to deal realistically with systemic racism. Instead, in my view, all he accomplishes is taking cheap shots at the people who are trying to help us understand this social malady. Systemic racism, for myriad reasons, is in the bedrock of American culture. McWhorter's assertion that wokeness is a religion has about as much credibility as his piece in *Forbes* in December of 2008, which declared that "Racism in America is Over."[34]

McWhorter's argument that Blacks can get beyond the confines of racism on their own is admirable, but unrealistic. Given that implicit racism is the evidence of brains working as they evolved to do, this biological reality must be thoroughly understood for there to be any viable efforts to stop it. I don't know anyone on this planet, other than some college professors, who is likely to know how bias works biologically and neurologically, together with anything close to an accurate account of racism in historical perspective. No one. Yet ignorance of our biological nature is tearing us apart.

What is happening now is a continuation of the nonsensical emotional battle in which the gist of the argument is based on who is accused of being a racist and who isn't. Not only will this age-old dispute be a waste of time, but it will also likely increase the ideological political distance between the left and right.

I can't resist writing this in italics, all caps, and underlined: *YOU DON'T HAVE TO BE A RACIST TO DO THINGS THAT HAVE A RACIST RESULT.* All we must do is make assumptions, give subconscious credence to the stigmas that we grew up with that have swayed our judgment just enough to make a difference, so that we treat those whom our subconscious has categorized as a *them* a little bit differently than we would have if we had perceived them to be one of us. We do this with intuition that comes to us in milliseconds via our subconscious. Then, if it feels a little politically incorrect when we say it out loud, we are fortunate to have been born to a species that can rationalize an opinion in the blink of an eye, so effectively that, too often we fool ourselves as to our reasons for having done so.

UNDERSTANDING POLITICS
IS IMPERATIVE

Understanding politics is essential, but criminal justice is not possible unless law enforcement is apolitical. But increasingly, law enforcement has become more and more politicized. The danger of this divide is hard to overestimate because confusing one's identity with law and order—we are the good guys, and those other folks aren't—is an extreme expression of tribalism. In other words, this is a stance in which *identity* can become the only thing that really seems to matter. When police officers become associated with a political party, justice is a casualty, because the law, or the question of right and wrong, becomes less important than whose side one appears to be on. Think about how this affects the psychology of jury duty. How are just verdicts even possible if us versus them becomes the core concern of law and order? The politicization of policing is how the cry for *law and order* came to be perceived as a dog-whistle crackdown on minorities. The subject of race must also be apolitical to have any chance that policing can lead to justice for the sake of justice. Police officers who strongly identify with a political party may automatically turn against a significant number of the citizens they are sworn to serve.

We are predisposed to be fond of the familiar, but just thinking our group is special doesn't make it so. Deeply deposited in the bedrock of all cultures is the inherent assumption that our group is more important and more virtuous than other groups by nature of who we are. If it were otherwise, our species might not have survived. Thus, politics contains strategies for supremacy whose primary ideology is, as often as not, buried deeply enough so as not to be obvious. For example, there are groups who assume their own natural dominance is threatened by calls for equality, because they believe their supremacy should be self-evident. Here we have as a prime example the view of the Confederacy that, while defeated during the American Civil War, is still alive and well more than a hundred and fifty years later, as what historian Heather Cox Richardson describes as "Movement Conservatism."[35] The cultural backlash underway to make the word *woke* a pejorative expression is steeped in Movement Conservatism. To be woke, in the minds of those who came up with the term, is to be enlightened. This includes the thesis of this book, which argues that we must acknowledge how our brains developed to keep us secure. Being woke doesn't require the demonization of anyone; it is about ridding humanity of a social scourge.

So, these anti-woke folks want to talk about religion. Let's do that. The smoldering resentment in the Deep South, called The Lost Cause, qualifies as being a religion by orders of magnitude more so than any effort to mitigate racial bias. In her book, *Jesus and John Wayne: How White Evangelicals Corrupted a Faith and Fractured a Nation*, historian Kristin Kobes Du Mez writes:

In the aftermath of the Civil War, the Lost Cause of the Confederate South had blended with Christian theology to produce a distinctly southern variation of civil religion, one that upheld Robert E. Lee as its patron saint. In this tradition, fundamentalist pastors like W. A. Criswell of First Baptist Dallas (Robert Jeffress's future home) crusaded against integration as 'a denial of all that we believe in.' To such opponents, civil rights activism was a sign of disruption and disorder; many denounced Martin Luther King, Jr. as a communist agitator.[36]

In his book, *Robert E. Lee and Me*, retired Brigadier General Ty Seidule, professor emeritus of history at West Point, has written a devastating take-down of Southern white supremacy. It is a searing indictment of the South's fantasized version of racial history. He describes a rebel force that chose armed rebellion because they would not accept the results of a democratic election. Sounds eerily familiar in our time. General Seidule writes:

> The Lost Cause became a movement, an ideology, a myth, even a civil religion that would unite first in the white South and eventually the nation around the meaning of the Civil War. The Lost Cause might have helped unite the country and bring the South back into the nation far more quickly than bloody civil wars in other lands. But this lie came at a horrible, deadly, impossible cost to the nation, a cost we are still paying today.[37]

He reminds his readers that the "flawed memory of the Civil War, formed the ideological foundation for white supremacy and Jim Crow laws."[38]

General Seidule grew up in the South with an abiding reverence for Southern history and affection for Robert E. Lee that at times seemed to emulate worship, until he began to unravel the propaganda. I grew up in similar circumstances, but my knowledge of history was not nearly as sophisticated as his was. I also grew up believing in a naïve version of the Lost Cause, based mostly on the assumption that most of the adults in my life knew what they were talking about. I suspect it took me longer to deconstruct my indoctrination than it did the General. I don't remember how the Texas public school textbooks in the 1950s treated the Civil War, but it is an easy guess that they minimized the role of slavery.

David W. Blight's description in *Race and Reunion: The Civil War in American Memory* captures the very heart of the subject. He writes:

> **The Lost Cause took root in a Southern culture awash in an admixture of physical destruction, the psychological trauma of defeat, a democratic Party resisting Reconstruction, racial violence, and with time, an abiding sentimentalism. On the broadest level, it came to represent a mood, or attitude toward the past. It took hold in specific arguments, organizations, and rituals, and for many Southerners it became a natural extension of evangelical piety, a civil religion that helped them link their sense of loss to a Christian conception of history. Like all great mythologies, the Lost Cause changed with succeeding generations and shifting political circumstances.[39]**

In *Baptized in Blood: The Religion of The Lost Cause, 1865-1920*, Charles Regan Wilson tells the story of how "baptized in blood" became a recurring rallying cry in the Post-Civil War period in the South as a vigorous effort to preserve Southern identity as an authentic religious sentiment, steeped in the ethos of white supremacy and with the spiritual authority of permanently establishing the Antebellum South as having been the pinnacle of human virtue. A vibrant residue of this sentimentality still resides in the South and the recent removal of Confederate icons that were monuments raised as belligerent acts of defiance has spawned a revival of Southern animosity.[40]

Robert E. Lee and Me examines many of the atrocities that occurred in the South during post-Reconstruction, along with Jim Crow laws, as well as the racist literature we grew up with. For example, Seidule writes:

> In *Gone with the Wind*, Reconstruction is evil. Mitchell writes a thumping declaration of counterrevolution. As Scarlett describes Reconstruction [quoting Scarlett from the novel], "Here was the astonishing spectacle of half a nation attempting, at the point of bayonet, to force upon the other half the rule of negroes, many of them scarcely one generation out of African jungles."[41]

Deep-seated feelings of resentment born in the Lost Cause took on a new life in the 1950s because of the fallout from Brown v. Board of Education. Enraged by the ruling of desegregation in Brown v. Board of Education, one James McGill Buchanan, an economist who would later win a Nobel Prize, developed an ideological strategy over decades that poses a lethal threat to democracy.[42]

Buchanan's work was born in white supremacy and steeped in the ethos of the Lost Cause, but over time, class supremacy and economic success as a measure of status became the central point in the movement, and thus, the underlying role of racism, although still relevant, was less obvious. The ideologues of this movement feel no sense of responsibility for the efforts and sacrifices of those who before them who made their success in life possible. They believe their wealth, no matter how it was acquired, means their debt to society is paid in full. These extremists believe working people are parasites and that taxes amount to theft. Their goal is to render the government incapable of restricting them in anything they do.

What Nancy Maclean shows in her book *Democracy in Chains* is how this anti-government ideology has wormed its way into our courts, laws, and state legislators, with enormous amounts of dark money support which increasingly results in voter suppression. The big question at this point is if this movement can still be stopped.

PREHISTORY

For thousands of generations, our hunter-gatherer ancestors lived in small groups, usually of a few dozen and seldom over 150.[43] During these times, mankind was on the dinner menu of large predators. Evolution favored those whose wariness of the unfamiliar equipped them to constantly check for warnings of possible harm up front, enabling them to act without hesitation in the case of danger. Those who survived were those who were quick to sense a threat of any kind, which makes perfect sense to a species that spent eons being stalked by predators or being killed by marauding tribes of strangers. But most of the time, our thinking about this subject, without acknowledging our evolutionary development, totally misperceives and misunderstands what we are up against. The threats have changed significantly, but our brains haven't.

I have spent an extraordinary amount of time trying to imagine what it was like for our ancestors before the development of language. Imagine spending every waking hour being hyper-alert because of the danger from beasts and warring strangers. I spent a couple of years in this endeavor in preparation for one of my fiction pieces and the subject has never been far from my mind since. Simply put, we are wired for being wary of all kinds of threats and all manifestations of the unfamiliar. We still have the same Stone Age biological predilections for being safe that were effective during prehistory, and we still apply them daily, although our circumstances have changed dramatically. But in some ways, life is more hazardous today. The dark web of cyberspace, for example, is analogous to the mostly hidden but always imminent dangers of the Serengeti Plain.

For thousands of generations, it has been practical to be suspicious of those people our subconscious has categorized as being different—just enough to be considered not one of us, not one of our 150. Yet as obvious as it is that our brains still work this way, we can't seem to get it through our heads what this means in practical terms. Arguing that because we don't feel any ill will towards the people our subconscious has categorized as being different than us, even enough to treat them slightly differently than those close to us, is just not realistic. First impressions about any and everything that could possibly pose a threat come to us milliseconds before our frontal cortex's conscious awareness even becomes actively alert.

In imagining what it was like before our species developed language, all we can do is guess and speculate, but when our kind had to warn family members of danger by grunting or making a noise or a gesture, I don't think it is out of the question to liken their everyday alertness to that of the extreme caution a deer exhibits when entering an open field. The reason our hair stands on end at times comes from unexpectedly facing unknowns. Life for our species used to be a precarious daily struggle because of so many large predators. Saber-toothed cats, for example, have only been extinct for about 10,000 years. Natural selection rewarded a sentinel awareness in human beings, and this is not something easily turned off. Moreover, when it comes to seeing something suspicious, our limbic system evolved to give safety the benefit of the doubt. Those who didn't take a chance had a better survival rate.

Fifty thousand years ago, killing a stranger you thought had a spear that turned out to be walking stick simply meant you were still alive and your progeny would have the chance to endure. Consider this, though, in terms of today, with a police officer's assumption about a shiny object in the hand of a suspicious person. If the officer doesn't control his or her limbic reflex, they may be legally held accountable under the assumption that they should have done so without any credence being given to the evolutionary benefit of betting big on the worst of circumstances. It is interesting to imagine oneself in that situation about fifty thousand years ago, then today as a peace officer. If you spend some time and effort imagining the ancient past, the difference in the imagined feelings of today may be insightful. We frame killing as wrong—it's part of our societal ethics—but would our Stone Age ancestors have felt the same way?

Mitigating our Stone Age predilections requires a thorough understanding of how our brains work and for us to be hyperaware in acknowledging bias when occasions arise that call for us to be morally objective. Doing this effectively requires being suspicious that our subconscious has inferred that there is some validity to the biases we have witnessed growing up, even if we didn't agree with them, then or now. Our subconscious is amoral. Its only objective is nailing reality to keep us safe, and it does this strictly based on appearances and subtle inferences.

Imagine that tomorrow the Yellowstone Super Volcano erupts and kills millions of people coast to coast. Government everywhere is nonexistent, desperate survivors hunt in gangs and violence over resources is relentless. Now, if you are a survivor, how are you going to feel when unexpectedly encountering strangers in these circumstances? Would we not, at least in matters of degree, be partway back to the Stone Age? After all, our biological equipment for living with such danger still works perfectly. Danger thousands of years ago was everywhere—weather, sounds, a scent on the wind, eating the wrong plant, taking the wrong path. That which was strange and unfamiliar was suspect, thus our limbic system evolved with a sentinel awareness dedicated to keeping us safe 24/7.

Now, stop here for a moment and ask yourself what would have been the case if our brains didn't evolve to favor the familiar. Would our species have survived if we weren't prone to be constantly alert, and, when it comes to dangerous circumstances of any kind, hyperaware?

Today, our circumstances have changed, but our brains haven't. Unless we are in the vicinity of man-eating beasts, we no longer need to worry that the snapping of a twig means a predator is about to pounce on us, although we are still likely to be startled hearing it. But we still face many risky circumstances—clicking on the wrong icon or URL on our cell phone or computer, being involved in road rage from not paying attention to other drivers or answering a call from an unknown number (trusting strangers can still be costly).

The list of possible dangerous encounters is longer and more complicated than in prehistory, yet our coping system hasn't changed. Would it not be surprising then, if we didn't jump to conclusions about whether we can trust strangers when we meet them? Here is the kicker: The evolution of human brains gave us a hardwired double standard when it comes to recognizing people who are unfamiliar. In every culture in the world, babies learn to discern intricate details in the faces of those they grow up with, which is precisely why many cultures believe other races of people all look alike.[44]

When meeting strangers on the Serengeti Plain, a better-safe-than-sorry estimation of whether they might pose a threat represented a shortcut survival advantage. Obviously, it is not as necessary just to stay alive as it was in prehistory, but we still use the same processes instinctively. As a species, we are wired to be wary and, in some ways, we face more threats than ever before.

The World Wide Web, regarding danger, is analogous to a banquet of treats and opportunities, goods and services almost beyond measure, with an invisible venomous spiderweb in the background. It is worth frequently reminding ourselves that we don't live in the natural world in which our cerebral biology evolved. Our world today is socially contrived and extremely complicated, and we experience stress levels that, compared with our ancestors' lives, were unlikely, especially regarding social status. Neuroscientist Robert M. Sapolsky puts this existential reality in clear social perspective: "When humans invented material inequality, they came up with a way of subjugating the low ranking like nothing ever before seen in the primate world."[45]

WE ARE BIOLOGICALLY
TRIBALISTIC

Oxytocin and Vasopressin

The human brain has been compared to a computer, so much so that a computation theory of mind is hard to escape, but in my view, it would be more accurate to acknowledge that we have a highly active chemical factory in our heads. The roles the neuropeptides oxytocin and vasopressin play in our pair-bonding and social relationships are fascinating. We have known about the bonding hormone oxytocin (often called the love hormone) for nearly a century, but recently, researchers at the University of Amsterdam discovered that this hormone is also a cause for tribalistic behavior, in that, at some mysterious point of experiencing too much otherness, it seems to trigger the impulse to ostracize.[46] Oxytocin seems to better enable us to recognize our own tribe and makes us very much aware of who is not of our group, so to speak.[47]

In *Behave*, Robert M. Sapolsky writes:

> Oxytocin and vasopressin facilitate mother-infant bond formation and monogamous pair bonding, decrease anxiety and stress, enhance trust and social affiliation, and make people cooperative and generous. But this comes with a huge caveat—these hormones increase prosociality only toward an Us. When dealing with Thems, they make us more ethnocentric and xenophobic. Oxytocin is not a universal luv hormone. It's a parochial one.[48]

Simply put, we seem chemically cocktailed for tribalistic behavior. Scandinavian countries that have a history of being generous and welcoming to outsiders have in recent years been rethinking their immigration policies, as they appear to have surpassed an *otherness* tipping point in which differences really matter.[49]

Limbic System

In *Blue Bias*, I characterized our limbic system, which contains our brain's major emotional regulating structures, consisting of the hypothalamus, the hippocampus, the amygdala, and the thalamus, as a sentinel awareness system for our personal safety.[50] The amygdala is capable of perceiving fear-evoking stimuli so subtle and fleeting that they are beneath conscious awareness.[51] When we see the face of a stranger, especially of another race, our amygdala is instantaneously activated. Our limbic system is preoccupied with keeping us safe: It evolved to warn us of threats in milliseconds, before our frontal cortex (our executive brain function) is even aware of the possibility of harm. In other words, limbic system warnings evolved out of necessity to enable us to act quickly without having to spend time thinking and reflecting about what we need to do. In a nutshell, we are equipped by evolution to be cautious of strangers and to jump to conclusions in milliseconds based on scant observations and subconscious memories.

So, when we consider how such a warning system would work effectively to keep us safe, it becomes clear that it would be necessary to learn from every experience we encounter in which danger or embarrassment of any kind might exist. And thus, our sentinel awareness system pays attention and records assumptions when our frontal cortex, our executive brain function, is not even aware that observations are being made. It is difficult to overemphasize the point that we are still equipped with the evolutionary gray matter that kept our primitive ancestors one step ahead of large predators on the Serengeti Plain. It makes perfect sense that our nervous system would evolve to be always alert and to make use of and benefit from everything we observe and experience. What makes this process problematic is that we internalize misperceptions as easily as we do correct assumptions. We will never be able to successfully address implicit racial bias until we understand how our minds work so thoroughly that we will be unable forget this biological behavioral predisposition when it matters. In our ancient past, there was often a greater risk in downplaying a potential danger than in exaggerating one. We still face many threats but few of them call for split-second life-and-death decisions. Today though, our subconscious biases embellish our opinions toward popular beliefs, regardless of whether or not we agree with those assumptions.

For a time, Sigmund Freud made the influence of the subconscious a front-page issue as being a primary motivating behavioral source, but much of what he got right has been neglected because he also got a lot of things wrong. Freud died in 1939, but throughout the 1940s, 50s, and 60s, his influence about the importance of the subconscious was mentioned frequently in movies and public discourse—especially Freudian slips, unintentional spoken errors which are suspected to reveal subconscious intent. My take is that the wholesale confusion about how bias works suggests Freud's insistence on the importance of our subconscious remains grossly understated. A thorough understanding of the way our subconscious influences us is necessary because it holds a key to our understanding the ever-present nature of unintentional bias or assumptions based on simple categorical observations that are completely without malice, but in which the results can be deadly, mimicking explicit racism.

Socialization

Growing up is when stereotyping and stigmatizing become navigational shortcuts so we can make good decisions. As noted, we are taught that stereotyping is inappropriate, so we deny doing it, although everyone does. The fact that we do this subconsciously, on automatic, so to speak, worsens our ability to think clearly about bias, and it jeopardizes the whole conversation about implicit bias and racism. In *The Anatomy of Racial Inequality*, Glenn C. Loury calls our generalizations "biased social cognition."[52]

In *Stigma: How We Treat Outsiders*, Gerhard Falk identifies the groups that came to mind when I was growing up in Oklahoma and Texas in the 1940s and 50s. Falk referred to these as being existential stigmas: the mentally ill, homosexuals, retarded (Falk's term) people, the exceedingly obese, the old, single women and Native Americans.[53] Reflect on your reaction to these groups today. Do you detect stigma still?

In her book *Caste*, Isabel Wilkerson tells us about a brilliant young man in the Dalit caste (an untouchable) raised in India who came to America, earning a Ph.D. at a prestigious East Coast university, who still to this day can't bring himself to breach the taboo of looking a member of the higher castes in his home country directly in the eyes.[54] Culturalization is powerful. We form biases about myriad subjects, and in addition to racial bias, our society is rife with biases against age, gender, obesity, class, and religious affiliation or a lack of it.

What would likely be the results if any group of an easily recognizable race of people were enslaved for centuries, and, upon release, reimprisoned in numbers of tens of thousands on made-up criminal charges solely for the purposes of exploiting their labor, then for generations were denied a whole range of opportunities in education, employment, loans for housing and business development, restricted via zoning regulations to live only in places readily identifiable as already being impoverished? Then overpoliced incessantly, sentenced to prison disproportionally, then having their disadvantaged communities targeted as a major source for funding local government, with revenue from summons, traffic fines, misdemeanors, and felonies—which amounts to funding government on the backs of the people who can least afford it? The stress of living under these conditions is an effective means of turning misdemeanors into felonies leading to mass prison incarnation—which is clearly based by default on race?

This is where stereotype meets stigma. Since our gray matter has already set the categorization up when we were growing up, then taking the next step in marking our shortcut navigation points for making our way in the world are set. Our ducks are aligned, so to speak. Linking a stereotype to a stigma is effortless. It will be in part a reasonable and rational assumption to believe that the people living in the conditions above are less trustworthy regarding credit, less employable, more likely to engage in criminal activity and more dangerous. But failing to understand that there are damned good reasons for a grain of truth being applied to citizens who have experienced this treatment is educational malpractice and it undermines the likelihood of public civility and social cohesion.

Cognitive scientist Paul Bloom reminds us that our views about not judging people solely based on their skin color is a modern insight, that "for most of human history, nobody saw anything wrong with racism."[55] Bias is what brains do: It's how we have survived as a species. We categorize and sort people, places, and things, from birth to death, and we are biologically predisposed to favor the familiar over that which is different. We readily recognize the faces of our own race and have difficulty distinguishing the faces of others. We grow up making assumptions about millions of circumstances, while forming opinions that we remain unaware of until we have a compelling reason to offer a judgment. If a race or group of people has been subject to stigma for centuries, it is almost impossible not to have been influenced.

This is so culturally forceful that even those who are stigmatized often internalize biases against their own race or group. Slavery, Jim Crow laws, separate but equal, legal redlining, and discrimination in healthcare and employment have resulted in the forced creation of low-income communities from coast to coast in which, from the very beginning of policing, the residents have experienced extraordinarily aggressive policing and harsher punishments by the courts. To ignore this history and claim that it has had no effect on the economic inequality experienced by African Americans is ludicrous.

My generation grew up with Shirley Temple movies, *Gone with the Wind*, and countless in-person examples of minorities in roles as subservient domestic workers. In America in the 1940s and 50s, children had good reason to believe that the people who lived in nice houses were mostly white, that nurses and schoolteachers were white women, and doctors, lawyers, and politicians were white men. It is a big mistake to conclude that this experience does not result in a subconscious worldview of assumptions about the implied virtue of being white and the stigma of being black or just decidedly different. Whatever kind of experience we are engaged in as we grow up leaves us with ambiguous assumptions and impressions that are, for all practical purposes, permanent because we do not have the knowledge to rewrite this life experience, or to overwrite our subconscious memories with their vast array of intuitive opinions only milliseconds away if we are called upon to offer an opinion.

The bottom line is that if we grow up in a culture where races or groups of people are stigmatized, we will have likely made notice and cemented the memory in gray matter. This is a reason so many people deny being racially biased, yet statistical analysis shows that we live in a society in which racial bias is ever-present and socially oppressive. If a race of people is consigned to domestic service for generations, then rationalizing about their not having the qualifications for more complex work can sound like common sense because it does make sense—but it isn't right, because it is the result of a preventable wrong. For truly concerned citizens, stereotypes and stigmas represent humanistic opportunities to think our way to a more morally mature civilization.

Groupishness

In *Why We're Polarized,* Ezra Klein said:

> **Human beings evolved to exist in groups. To be part of a group, and to see that group thrive, meant survival. To be exiled from a group or to see your group crushed by its enemies, could mean death. Is it really so strange that we evolved to feel the life-and-death stakes of group belonging and status?**[56]

We frequently call attention to the fact that we are social creatures when we come together as groups in myriad ways, through geography (as in location), our interests, our fates, our likes and dislikes, our blood relations and religious affiliations, and for about any reason we can convince others to join with us in a common cause. Think about how eager we are to adopt a favorite in team sports, which will render us partially incapable of being fair about judging penalty calls against our teams by the referees.

Crowds evoke a memetic effect in that their presence implies something is up—something to see, maybe, something to do. Thus, movements, political parties, religious efforts, associations, clubs, and even mobs all have the potential for arousing a bandwagon effect of climbing on board. This applies to a vast range of activities, but nothing quite compares to the fervor of enlistment when the driving force is hatred. It only takes a seed of contempt to get the process of ideological amplification underway in full swing. When the Black Lives Matter Movement began to call attention to the murder of George Floyd and the crowds became unruly, Donald Trump threatened to send Army troops to stop the protests and it ignited a racist backlash against the Black Lives Matter Movement that caught fire and still smolders today.

Bias is What Brains Do

If the groups we belong to have biased opinions about shape, size, gender, gender roles, accents, sexual orientation, ambition, addiction, immigration, icons and symbols, media, age, marriage, fidelity, violence, divorce, psychology, siblings, tradition, clothing, skin color, hairstyle, cleanliness, homosexuality, friendship, the American Dream, art, family, philosophy, heroics, motherhood, illness, single motherhood, slavery, depression, identity, vegetarianism, college degrees, civil rights, medical marijuana, science, prostitution, discipline, traffic regulations, honor, rehabilitation, animal welfare, climate change, parental authority, wages, homelessness, welfare, gangs, mental illness, the supernatural, intellectual disability, prison, death, manual labor, cruelty, citizenship, poverty, vocation, compassion, public service, forgiveness, drugs, education, achievement, physical fitness, crime and punishment, retirement, good and evil, jury duty, tolerance, loyalty, advertising, social status, social class, Social Security, Medicare, private insurance, purity and sanctity, alcohol, criminals, obesity, justice, public health care, elections, music, tradition, genocide, patriarchy, religion, race, child development, work, punishment, economics, discrimination, sexism, urbanization, police, wealth, authoritarianism, artificial intelligence, digital technology, military service, socialism, capitalism, civility, fair play, democracy, ethics, tribalism, private property, movies, food, war, charity, etiquette, friendship, patriotism, virtue—and the list could go on for many more pages, because *it is hard to make the point effectively* without showing the gravity of subjects our subconscious has made note of and will regurgitate on cue as intuition if the need arises—we will have opinions that likely mirror those of the groups we grew up with.

For most of us, by the time we are adults, we have adamant biases about many of the subjects above, along with a whole host of subconscious assumptions that will only surface if we are called upon to offer judgment. The role our subconscious plays in all these subjects and too many more to list is often analogous to our having done a sloppy job of photoshopping our life experience. I say "sloppy" because many intuitive conclusions our subconscious has assumed to be correct are casual observations that are half-baked at best. We jump to conclusions based on scant information and, because we don't follow through, we are left with internalized assumptions that were misplaced to begin with.

If our fellow citizens collectively have distinct opinions about these issues, our subconscious minds will have made note. We are astute observers, paying attention without realizing that we are paying attention. We begin this hyperawareness as children as we learn without being aware that we are learning. A prime example is the oft-referenced story of a little white girl who, upon seeing an African American baby girl, told her mother to look at the baby maid. Pretending that we are in general totally unbiased when it comes to race or ethnicity is patently absurd, yet we still hear the argument about our judicial system, and about judges specifically, claiming that they are unbiased.

Sadly, the evidence is clear that many judges don't understand how their own minds work when it comes to rendering opinions. It is commonplace for judges to claim they are bias-free, then have their appointments supported or opposed precisely because the public already assumes how their seemingly known ideological biases are likely to affect their rulings. Often, judges are appointed who are thought to be biased toward interpreting the law as written, but instead their view of written law is subordinate to their political positions. To adopt any aspect of this ethos as a political posture in law enforcement is to undermine the aspiration *to protect and serve*. While every police officer is entitled to his or her right to vote for their political convictions, politics has no place on the street because an "us versus them" ideology is thus inevitable. We are well equipped to make distinctions without understanding the political significance of what is implied in the bedrock of the issue at hand. In other words, we often act in haste.

Every American has a right to their political opinion and a right to vote, regardless of their occupational duties. But police officers, like our military, must be apolitical in carrying out their service. Police unions that jump on a political bandwagon for any party beyond advocating for better benefits and working conditions for their officers diminish their ability to be believed as being just for justice's sake. Wearing politics on one's sleeve in public service is analogous to having a chip on one's shoulder. In my view, police misconduct should not be adjudicated with union representation but by the very same justice system that everyone else must abide by. Increasingly, the primary influence of police unions is to keep unfit officers on the job—an anathema to the oath to protect and serve.

As stated earlier, when we encounter strangers or members of groups we have subconsciously identified as "others," if we are acting without the intense intervention of our frontal cortex, we are left to respond "primitively" to the situation. In other words, unless a police officer shifts gears by deliberately forcing the executive function of their frontal cortex to take over the interaction they are engaged in, then it will likely continue as it began: with a first impression based on a subconscious intuition.

Consider this analogy: Jim grew up in a racist community and he was adamant about paying close attention to what was going on around him. He doesn't want James to be surprised, hurt, or embarrassed.

James is clearly disturbed by all expressions of racism. Jim comes to his aid, offering intuitive advice to explain racism in realistic and rational terms. Jim has been trying hard all his life, 24/7, to peg reality to keep James safe. Jim pays attention to anything and everything that may prove dangerous or embarrassing to James, and he warns him instantaneously when necessary.

You see, Jim and James are the same person. Jim is James's subconscious. Jim and James are on different communication frequencies, and James does not have direct programming access to the vast repertoire of assumptions Jim has carefully stored, so they just communicate as best they can. When subjects involving race call for an opinion, James accepts Jim's rationalizations eagerly because they always sound exceptionally plausible, even though they are often subtle examples of learned bias. James believes Jim and has little reason to suspect that Jim is biased because he sounds so convincing.

Creating and establishing an internal database of knowledge that becomes our worldview is analogous to building a barn one board at a time. Evolution wired us with the ability to discern the fine details and uniqueness of the faces of our respective race or group of individuals we grow up with, which, as has been mentioned, is why other races of people seem to all look alike. This predilection is like putting a board on a framed wall and starting a long nail. Each subsequent action that we observe subconsciously acts as a hammer strike on the nail. If we grow up and a race of people is treated disparagingly and is only allowed low-paying jobs, working as domestic servants or as laborers, for example, and if they are depicted as being untrustworthy and inclined to break the law, then each instance of this type of observation adds another board and a nail. By the time we are adults, we have internalized a huge barn, so well-built and reinforced that, for most practical purposes, it will be indestructible. Thus, this metaphorical example should assume our being incapable of impartiality; when asked to make a conscious decision about any subject in which we have a barn's worth of assumptions, it is inescapably difficult if not impossible without strenuous effort to be fair.

There is tremendous confusion about the essence of racial bias. Most of it is because we fail to acknowledge how evolution has equipped us to safely navigate our daily experience. It is hard to overstate the case that we are biologically predisposed to be suspicious of strangers because we are exceptionally prone to favor that which is familiar. In *The Hidden Brain*, Shankar Vedantam puts this in perspective: "Our blindness to bias seems willful—until you remember that the central feature of unconscious bias is that it is unconscious."[57] Our categorizing, in the sense of "us versus them," is not something that we have conscious control over. Our brains have been doing this for all our lives simply to make sense of what is before us.

It is interesting to imagine all our subconscious memories strung together in algorithmic form, and when we encounter situations in which we need the essence of this knowledge, they come to us as flashes of instinctual insight condensed to a feeling of intuition. The instances of some of our experiences dealing with racial prejudices and stereotypes could be pages long—so many that it is very idealistic to imagine that the extent of this life experience won't have any influence at all on our gut-level opinions, that something to do with race could come to us metaphorically as noted by a colossal barn's worth of life experience. Consider that in every circumstance we face, we have the benefit of an algorithmic life experience cobbled together from our subconscious, based upon what are at times barely more than illusions that will offer instinctive nudges toward the implied reality that our life experience suggests is the case.

Neuroimaging

A stereotype is a generalization, an accepted estimation of those usually considered outsiders to the observer based on cultural suspicion that may be reasonably probable but very well may not apply in specific cases. We stereotype automatically.[58] If not for our ability to ostracize for otherness, we would be incapable of bonding. We begin as infants, sorting and categorizing everything we see, hear, and touch to make sense of the world, and only death will stop us. In his book *Why We Snap*, neuroscientist R. Douglas Fields explains how neuroimaging clearly shows that racial prejudice and stereotyping are wired into our brains as a means of learning. Fields reports that, "Prejudice and stereotypes appear to alter early events in the brain involved in face processing"—and that out-group members are often viewed as being threatening, thus requiring our vigilance.[59] Gordon W. Allport speculated that "Overcategorization is perhaps the commonest trick of the human mind."[60] We must categorize because our perception is based on metaphor. We understand everything by comparison to something else, something known, to something else, again and yet again.

Numerous studies explain how, as infants, we become astute observers of the facial features of our relatives, with the ability to easily recognize individuals of our own racial groups, but we remain somewhat flummoxed when it comes to recognizing individuals of other races, which is where the common slang of *they all look alike* is shown to contain a kernel of truth.[61]

Kind-sight and Identity Crazed

In *Us and Them: The Science of Identity,* David Berreby calls our attention to what he calls *kind-sight,* making the case that grouping people into categories is an inborn trait that is both involuntary and automatic and "can't be shut off." He says, "It's not evil, it's not good. It's just there, a mental facility we can't help using, with rules different from the ones used by other parts."[62] We humans are quick to distinguish race. In *Behave: The Biology of Humans at Our Best and Worst,* Robert M. Sapolsky writes, "We may claim to judge someone by the content of their character rather than by the color of their skin. But our brains sure as hell note the color, real fast."[63] Sapolsky points out that infants learn to distinguish faces of their race early on and that if they seldom see faces of another race, then a different color than their own will be salient.[64] When it comes to our feelings about others not of our respective groups, we don't even need to talk about our differences: Our facial expressions and body language are enough to subtly announce that we are justified in distancing ourselves from those whom we have intuitively categorized as the *other* to any degree, and for any reason.

In an essay in *Edge,* evolutionary psychologist John Tooby argues that our coalitional instincts are so pronounced that "we project coalitions into everything, even where they have no place, such as in science. We are identity-crazed."[65] Tooby suggests that the primary function that drives the evolution of coalitions is the amplification of power that comes with coalition membership. So, equipped with kind-sight and a penchant for being obsessively focused on identity, the inherent difficulty in navigating and negotiating our differences with those we have subconsciously categorized as the others should be coming into focus as an evolved brain predilection that needs to be amended. Or put another way, our Stone Age biological software needs a malware patch to cope with modernity. Stereotypes and stigmas need to spark yellow warning lights in our mind to *think this through.*

Thinking Fast and Slow

A little over four decades ago, Israeli psychologists Daniel Kahneman and Amos Tversky discovered the functioning of our limbic alarm system by essentially reverse-engineering our decision-making processes. Daniel Kahneman's book, *Thinking, Fast and Slow,* explains how this works.[66] Thinking fast, which Kahneman describes as System One, stems from our subconscious memory. It is on the same frequency as our limbic alarm system. Thinking slow, which he describes as System Two, is the work of the executive function of our frontal cortex. System One, fast thinking, is automatic: We have very little control over it, so it is easy to appreciate how bias works, especially when we are not paying close attention and using slow thinking to closely examine what we are experiencing. Fast thinking, in the case of potential harm, is limbic based, it's intuitive, while slow thinking is more logically analytical. Fast thinking comes to us from the residue of stored memory, as Kahneman writes, "This is how the remembering self works: it composes stories and keeps them for future reference."[67]

When you apply fast and slow thinking to the work of a police officer, for example, or to anyone in a profession which regularly encounters emergencies, it is useful to appreciate the notion that each person's limbic system works as a silent partner in framing each encounter on the job as having been emotionally introduced through a subconscious warning in which caution may be warranted because of the potential for harm. The categories above are slam-dunk clues that we evolved biologically to jump to conclusions because doing so increased our chances for survival in a wild and savage world, a world red in tooth and claw in which suspicion was always the best bet.

The Frailties of Human Judgment

In their book *Noise: A Flaw in Human Judgment*, Daniel Kahneman, Oliver Sibony, and Cass R. Sunstein address the difficulty of making clear objective observations and decisions because of all the interferences that are likely to muddle our thinking, especially when it comes to context—the circumstances we find ourselves in when we make decisions. These authors call these myriad kinds of impediments to clear thinking, and they make the point that all disciplines where accuracy matters are noisy.[68]

When my generation was growing up, we were taught that each of us had something called character and that this was a kind of an existential trademark, a statement to the world about who we are and what we stand for, by our being dependable and virtuous in our behavior. Unfortunately, we weren't warned that what we have tried to establish as our character when it comes to our being reliably consistent only works when we are paying attention. In other words, when we have shifted cerebrally into System Two thinking. We didn't know then, as so many still don't know now, that the circumstances we find ourselves in when we are going along on automatic, so to speak, in System One and not paying close attention to what we are doing or thinking, that things like our mood, the weather, the time of day, whether we are in a hurry, or hungry, afraid, or angry, in what neighborhood or environment we are in, or how we are feeling, or who is with us, and how familiar we are with them matters a lot. What research tells us is that circumstances fog our thinking, so to speak, and instead of bias, this qualifies as *noise*.

Take judges, for example. Who would have suspected that judges are more likely to give a harsher sentence on Monday, if their favorite sports team lost over the weekend, that they might be more lenient on their birthday, or that migrants may be less likely to be granted asylum if it is very hot outside?[69] There are so many research studies showing how context influences our behavior in ways that we would never have suspected unless we are made aware of them. Add implicit biases and the difficulty of being objective in all matters where judgment is required is rendered much more complicated than most of us would have suspected. When we begin with an intuitive thought, it can be hard to shift gears. As the authors of *Noise* explain, "In general, we jump to conclusions, then stick to them. We think we base our opinions on evidence, but the evidence we consider and our interpretation of it are likely to be distorted, at least to some extent, to fit our initial snap judgment."[70]

Colorblindness

Achieving a colorblind society seems like a worthy goal, but efforts have been extremely inconsistent. In her book, *The New Jim Crow: Mass Incarceration in the Age of Colorblindness*, Michelle Alexander shows that today, it is legal to discriminate against African Americans using all the past traditionally prejudiced methods, because all it takes is to label them criminals. She writes:

> Once you're labeled a felon, the old forms of dis-
> crimination—employment discrimination, housing
> discrimination, denial of the right to vote, denial of

50

educational opportunity, denial of food stamps and other public benefits, and the exclusion from jury service—are suddenly legal. As a criminal, you have scarcely more rights, and arguably less respect, than a black man living in Alabama at the height of Jim Crow. We have not ended racial caste in America, we have merely redesigned it.[71]

Alexander further states that "The deeply flawed nature of color-blindness, as a governing principle, is evidenced by the fact that the public consensus supporting incarceration is officially colorblind."[72] She argues that our commitment to being colorblind blinds us to "the existence of racial caste in America."[73]

If people who do not understand the influence of our subconscious, the nature of implicit bias and how our brains function via System One and System Two, pretend to be colorblind, then it is full speed ahead for implicit bias. Those who feel no animosity toward minorities, but who follow unspoken tradition, will continue to discriminate, and only those who have been wronged will be the wiser. Imagine what it would have been like in 1865, trying to explain how our subconscious is paying attention when we aren't, so to speak, and that paying attention is a key to overcoming unacknowledged tradition based on unreflective assumptions and misunderstood appearances.

The Hawthorne Effect

In the 1920s and 30s, Western Electric conducted studies intended to determine if better lighting could improve the productivity of employees in manufacturing. There were similar attempts to improve productivity by providing background music for workers. Remember elevator music and background music in department stores? These were attempts to influence employees and customers. What was ultimately determined was that better lighting or good background music were not what was resulting in improved productivity. The impetus for improving employee productivity was positively affected simply when employees were aware that their activities were being observed, titled the Hawthorne Effect. In other words, just knowing that people were paying attention to their behavior caused them to pay more attention to what they were doing. I can't help but wonder if the Hawthorne Effect is evidence that System Two thinking can be subtly influenced by an observer effect.[74]

THE POLICING DOUBLE
STANDARD

James Baldwin observed that history is persistently a part of the present.[75] Indeed, dig beneath the surface of any culture and we discover people engaged in behavioral traditions, the reasons for which are long forgotten. We celebrate holidays without fully appreciating the significance of their origins, and we wear clothing born of fashions no longer remembered or recognized. We engage in all sorts of activities, doing this or that, simply because this is the way it—whatever that is—has always been done.

A few centuries ago, white superiority and social dominance were accepted by most people as a harsh but fully justifiable reality. White racial superiority was considered common sense. Historians celebrate the Enlightenment as a clarion call for reason, but they seldom point out that most enlightened thinkers from this period believed deeply in white supremacy.[76]

So, when the first police forces were established in America, the sentiments and attitudes from the days of slavery and colonialism and the acceptance of white supremacy were a given. Thus, a double standard in policing didn't need to be discussed—it was simply considered a practical solution to an obvious social reality. That it was ill-conceived was not up for discussion because the political power to forcibly push back did not exist.

I am thoroughly acquainted with the double standard in policing, because in the 1960s, I was a participant. Due to my upbringing, I didn't understand it as a double standard then, but I do today. I am fully aware that it still exists, and it is not rare, but commonplace. In *The Broken Heart of America: St. Louis and the Violent History of the United States*, historian Walter Johnson, in discussing a housing project in St. Louis in the 1960s, quotes a memoir of a former St. Louis police officer's description of the Pruitt-Igoe project. He said, "it was commonplace to refer to Black migrants from the South as *Swamp Turkeys* and to Pruitt-Igoe as a *cesspool of humanity*, a *living nightmare*, a *combat zone* and inevitably, *Fort Apache*"[77] (Italics mine). You have only to read the Department of Justice's Ferguson Report of March 2015 to realize that this kind of attitude is still common among law enforcement officers in some departments.[78]

Evolution wired us for a tribalistic approach to life. For police officers, this means your tribe must include everyone. Being an ex-cop with an insatiable interest in the subject of race relations and biases, my position in this conflict is to vigorously avoid the unproductive and senseless back-and-forth arguments about whether racial bias exists, and to explain how it works in terms of our biological nature. And for policing, I am calling attention to a historic double standard in the treatment of African Americans by police officers that for the most part is just blindly accepted as tradition, as this is how we police in what are likely to be low-income Black and Latino communities. Moreover, some police officers on active duty today are indeed overtly racist in the traditional hateful sense and the politics of late have helped to feed this acrimony tremendously. But I firmly believe that most police officers simply relate to people not of their race as being different—different enough to be treated differently, albeit slightly, and this can indeed still be enough to tip the scales of judgment and treat them as members of an out-group. Or put more aptly, assuming the gleam in their hand is a weapon instead of a cell phone. It is, after all, not naïve to assume that we would give a member of our family or closely associated group the benefit of the doubt in such a case.

The history of how Black people are treated in this country by police officers is horrific and so much worse than is commonly believed. I know this firsthand, from having been a participant in applying the double standard and from having grown up internalizing white superiority, which was simply accepted as common sense in my region of the country at the time. I have spent years studying and researching the history of policing and if you will do likewise, unless you are a sociopath, you will become numb and fatigued by disgust from the myriad of examples so morally repulsive that you must take long breaks to keep going. My experience in doing this makes it exceptionally hard to listen to those who criticize the study of Critical Race Theory without losing my temper. Most of the people who do this have no appreciation of the horrid history that is beyond the reach of whitewashed textbook history. For the most part, these critics have no earthly idea what Critical Race Theory actually is and the term is simply used to reflect revulsion and disgust.

There are correlated elements involved in the double-standard treatment that African Americans experience by law enforcement.

55

One element is ensconced in tradition: It's related to the same mentality in which a training officer tells a rookie to forget what they learned in the police academy because "this is how we do it here." Minority communities have been policed more aggressively than affluent neighborhoods since the very first officer donned a uniform. Any seasoned police officer, when asked and given time to think it over, if they are being honest, will admit that it is tradition. Many may not likely acknowledge that a major reason for the longevity of the practice is rooted in the fact that these communities have traditionally lacked the economic and political power to push back forcefully enough to stop the practice. Every interested person should read the Department of Justice's Ferguson Report of March 2015. And don't kid yourself that similar aggressive and immoral policing doesn't still exist today in many American communities.[79]

That we have some overtly racist police officers in uniform today is a certainty, and they urgently need to be fired for being unfit for public service. My focus is on the behavior of well-meaning police officers who, while not intending to let their past subconscious assumptions wrongly influence their behavior, nevertheless exhibit the influence of implicit biases. I don't want us to get so distracted by an ideological battle that is likely to get us nowhere that we don't see what is at stake.

Explicit bias aside, most instances of racial bias in policing, in my view, have more to do with socialization and how our minds work than whether we are conscious racists. New sparkplugs won't help fix your car if the problem is a bad radiator hose. If our sole focus is on what is in our conscious minds, and we ignore the influence of our subconscious, we are similarly flummoxed. Contempt, animosity, and hatred are not necessary to consider a person "the other" when "the other" merits different treatment. In a nutshell, the double standard in the treatment of minorities by police officers has less to do with hatred than with the simple cerebral categorization that defaults automatically to our subconscious when we aren't paying attention. The key to mitigating implicit bias in policing is thoughtfulness on steroids. Caring about doing so is crucial to getting it done.

Racism is such a difficult social problem that eliminating racial prejudice is for the most part a manic social goal, with so much censure that almost no one wants to admit they are guilty of harboring racial animosity. Yet incidents of overt racial bias are frequently front-page media subjects. What we haven't understood until recently, for the umpteenth time, is that our limbic system acts as a biological sentinel alarm that front-loads our life experience with warnings of potential physical harm or embarrassment in milliseconds, well before our frontal cortex (our executive brain function) is even aware of what is transpiring.[80] Beyond physical harm, the historical cost of social humiliation was sometimes lethal.

Abject racism aside, most people don't want to be racially prejudiced, yet our brains have already done the subconscious sorting that categorizes people in an "us versus them" fashion. Brains categorize—this is how we tell boys from girls, men from women, police from security guards, bus drivers from passengers, sailors from soldiers, and coyotes from wolves. Neuroimaging shows that we do this early on, automatically, without an awareness that we have done so.[81] Think of how evolution would need to equip persons to remain safe in a world filled with large predators and warring neighbors only a few miles away. Such preparation would mean first things first, with caution and suspicion up front, which is precisely how our biology currently works. For most of humanity's existence on the planet, it was wise to be wary of strangers and to be always on alert for danger. We still have this predilection intact, although the dangers we face have lessened and changed their context.

All it takes to treat someone differently, using a different standard, is to see them as the *other*, in any context. Hatred or conscious animosity is not necessary to do this, yet the result can be just as damaging as if real hatred were present. To have any hope of eliminating harmful discrimination, we must stop making this an issue about whether we are overtly prejudiced and simply face up to the fact that evolution has wired us to pay remarkably close subconscious attention to every scenario that could result in harm, which includes anything and everything that seems unfamiliar. Rest assured, our gray matter has already taken care of this without our knowledge, when we were toddlers. This harsh reality has a tremendous impact on our nervous system and our brain development.

Implicit bias is not a rare phenomenon. Bias facilitates learning. Being cautious and conservative in our sentinel awareness makes evolutionary sense, but we need to adjust for modernity. We are no longer on the Serengeti Plain in Africa scanning the horizon for man-eating beasts. Yet strangers, uncertainty, and otherness still trigger our fast-thinking limbic system to take the slightest applicable cues from our experience as a need for caution. Police officers whose work is often dangerous need to know when to override their sentinel system, when executive thinking is called for, and they need to be so well trained in what to do in emergencies that they can act without thinking. In other words, they must rehearse for action with the need to think about what they need to do next, precisely when there won't be time to think.

People who attend diversity training who don't think it will benefit them prove the point with their attitude. If you don't think you are biased because you don't consciously feel a bias, and you can't be persuaded otherwise, instead of becoming more tolerant and objective about the ubiquity of implicit bias, you are likely to become even more adamant about claiming you are unbiased. For diversity training to work, it requires that participants genuinely care about learning how our minds work and learning that one does not need to hate or disdain others to have the same negative effect as if they did hate them: All one must do is to see them as being different and, accordingly, treat them as being different.

This means that our biases are not a sign of our poor characters; they are instead simply the way brains have tried to prepare us to live in a dangerous world. The circumstances of our lives have changed radically, but our brains haven't. Unfortunately, because we are not taught how this works, we are likely to spend an extraordinary amount of time denying the reality of what our brains have naturally assumed is the case, and the confusion goes downhill from there. Religious instruction can short-circuit the wherewithal to figure out what is going on here, because it makes no allowance for the subconscious, insisting instead that our conscious minds are in total control of our behavior.

If we follow the evidence in neuroscience, which reveals through neural imaging that categorizing and otherizing is something our limbic system does automatically on its own, and if we then use our frontal cortex to intervene, thus compensating for our having something akin to a photoshopped subconscious, we can mitigate implicit biases with an awareness that special attention is needed, like a flashing yellow caution light that unbiased frontal cortex judgment is needed here.

When we are called upon to make decisions and judgments in which bias is known to be a concern, to deal with them effectively, we must be hyperaware of what we are up against. We must engage our frontal cortex and think through the issue we are dealing with by being exceptionally thoughtful. And before you tell me that in your case it doesn't count, because you didn't grow up with any Black people present or that your parents taught you to respect everyone, this is just nonsense. Indeed, if one's community while growing up is all white, it may in fact increase the likelihood of seeing African Americans and other ethnicities as the *other*. If we grow up in a racially prejudiced culture, even the people who are discriminated against are likely to internalize some of the humiliation, which will include bias. Racial bias is built into our entertainment and literature and its ubiquity makes it hard to detect because it just seems like reality.

That global cinema gives us movies and dramas that depict Black men as being exceptionally dangerous is a given. If an unconscious implicit bias is what prompted an officer to select someone for a traffic stop, a bias the officer is unaware that he or she even has, then the following encounter with the person stopped will likely to continue in the frame or context of that bias. In his book, *How To Be An Antiracist*, Ibram X. Kendi writes about how Black children are so often treated like adults by the police, while adults are treated like children.[82] This observation rings painfully true with my experience, and I have no doubts that it still applies today in many places. In psychologist Jennifer Eberhardt's book *Biased: Uncovering the Hidden Prejudice that Shapes What We See, Think, and Do,* she describes an examination of nearly a thousand traffic stops conducted between 2015 and 2017 by 245 police officers in Oakland, California, and how, from the transcripts where the researchers isolated more than 36,000 utterances in greetings and statements, they enabled a computer program to identify the fact that the officer had stopped an African American, simply by the disrespect in the way the officer was addressing the person.[83]

Every police officer could benefit from carefully examining their own bodycam footage on a regular basis to see if they are exhibiting a bias by being disrespectful of minorities, or of gender, age, neighborhood, or other criteria. No one needs this kind of information more than officers who are being guided by unrecognized subconscious influences. Learning about this at an early period in one's career in law enforcement can be critical to one's ultimate success or failure as a police officer. I would not be a bit surprised that someday in the distant future, body cameras may help officers judge the level of threat they are facing and may even be capable of reminding officers when they cross the lines by seeming to disrespect someone because of a bias.

A more aggressive standard of policing in low-income minority neighborhoods represents historical reality.[84] No one needs to talk about this; it is simply an unspoken tradition. When I hear officers complain that the Black Lives Matter movement is without merit, all it does is reveal to me that they do not know the history of policing in this country, which, when it comes to the treatment of African Americans, is miles south of dreadful. There is simply no other way to explain it. Centuries of oppressive racial discrimination have left an indelible imprint on American culture, especially on the psyche of African Americans. "Two and a half centuries of slavery, 90 years of Jim Crow laws, 60 years of separate but equal, two generations of legal redlining followed by illegal redlining" where possible ever since, and the result is visible coast to coast in low-income communities with populations of Black and Brown people.[85] And those who believe that these communities were formed by something other than the oppression caused by these practices are willfully blind. Moreover, any attempt to objectively review the history of policing in these neighborhoods must conclude that a double standard in the treatment of the citizens in these communities has existed since the first officer donned a uniform. The history of policing in America specifically regarding racial issues is undeniably horrific and a thorough understanding of the past is the only way police officers can truly appreciate why the citizens in ethnic neighborhoods view them with so much distrust. We are an intensively tribalistic species and we are always subconsciously alert for degrees of difference that constitute a kind of otherness that warrants exceptional but subtle alertness and distrust.

We still have police officers attending bias training who resent being made to do so because they don't believe the training applies to them. As stated earlier, the only way bias instruction will work is if the trainees care about the matter and sincerely believe in the preparation. Neuroscientist David Eagleman argues that our brain distributes resources according to what we deem important, and for police officers, unacknowledged hidden bias can be a career-ender.[86] But until there is a widespread public understanding of how bias works and acknowledgement that this is not simply a policing problem, we will not be able to achieve substantial progress in mitigating implicit bias.

WHAT DOES ALL OF
THIS MEAN?

What can we deduce about our behavior concerning biases from all the information above? From prehistory, we learn that we are wired to be wary. From the biological chemical factory in our heads, we learn that we are chemically predisposed for tribalistic behavior. We are preconditioned to be comfortable with the familiar, and we can tolerate only so much otherness before we begin to ostracize. Our hyper sentinel limbic system frontloads our life experience so that we become aware of the things we are suspicious of or fear, even before we have the time to think carefully about what is occurring. Our brains use bias as a navigational tool, putting caution up front in milliseconds. We know through neuroimaging that our brain has taken care of categorization and stereotyping when we were very young and that we are exceptionally partial to our own kind. When we add kind-sight and Daniel Kahneman's and Amos Tversky's observations about thinking fast and slow, suddenly all of this makes perfect sense. Just as the Hawthorne Effect suggests, we may be able to be nudged to be more thoughtfully aware if we know we are being observed. Then, to take our evidence further, apply the concept of noise to the myriad reasons human judgment misfires, and the weight of these observations begins to paint a mental picture of why the subject of race in a cultural context is so difficult to people who haven't studied it intently.

What doesn't add up is why this information is not already considered common knowledge. Why haven't our behavioral professionals laid this out so that the cause and effect is clear? It doesn't take a puzzle master to reach the logical conclusions that the accumulated evidence listed above calls for. I can't help but wonder if intense political sensitivity is what has stood in the way of unraveling this dilemma which I can only characterize as having been an open secret for decades. Sometimes the hardest things to fully deconstruct and comprehend are what seem most obvious, but the centuries-long horrific history of racial bias in America urgently begs a solution. Taken independently, the categories above don't tell us very much about ourselves, but when you consider all of them together, they are, in my view, compelling evidence of the human tendency for tribalistic behavior, which should help explain why racial bias is a default predilection unless we are armed intellectually against its omnipresence. It will require continuous communal care and thoughtfulness to help put an end to it. To date, most of the social angst we experience in denying that we are racists because we have no ill feelings toward other races totally misses the point about how our brains evolved to be hyperalert for what were for eons, damned good reasons. Given all the examples above, it should be clear that evolution made racism inevitable, but we are still well equipped to mitigate its negative effects but for the will to do so.

Now, add noise and context to the difficulty in seeing and recognizing implicit bias and we are likely to witness a cascading effect. For example, the authors of *Noise* give examples of forensic scientists who, upon hearing that a suspect is for sure guilty of the evidence that they are examining to connect them to the crime, are more likely to let the bias influence their work.[87] Add context algorithmically, for example: mood, time of day, location, weather, race, gender, and numerous other environmentally contextual things to contend with and you'll see how messy this is. But this brings us to the kicker. We know now that, in our brains, our subconscious categorizing was completed before we knew enough about the subject of bias to even give it serious consideration. If we pretend to be colorblind, all we accomplish is allowing ourselves to cruise along on automatic pilot with System One thinking, without feeling the need to shift gears when it is important to do so. We should be able to appreciate the fact that once we have relegated any person as being different enough to be considered the *other* in any context, it becomes exceptionally easy to link this otherness to a social stigma which has the effect of setting the bias in stone. It will take a jackhammer's worth of thoughtful attention to overcome it. In *The Anatomy of Racial Inequality*, Glenn C. Loury writes, "*Discrimination is about how people are treated; stigma is about who, at the deepest level, they are understood to be* (italics his).[88] I disagree on a minor but major point. A stigma can indeed be deep, but it needn't be so far reaching at all. The slightest sense of association can apply, especially when the target has already been categorized as the *other*. Just as a deep feeling of bias is not necessary to cause a racist result, neither are racial animus or ill feelings necessary to believe in a stereotype or a clearly false assumption about a group or race of people so that one takes actions that are clearly racist. Relating to the *other* can easily become extreme because, after categorization has occurred, the path to extremes is clear of all contrary obstacles.

So, my take is that discrimination is about how people are treated; stereotyping is how people are broadly categorized; and stigma is for when the categorization connects and turns negative. We have briefly reviewed how African Americans have been historically oppressed in so many ways as to find a significant number of them living in comparatively impoverished communities, locations likely called high-crime areas, with policing that is more aggressive than in upper-class neighborhoods. In this environment, a stereotype draws obvious assumptions: STIGMA. People living in these neighborhoods, identified because of the color of their skin, are often stigmatized as lacking education, being unreliable, lacking skills, being lazy, being poor credit risks, being drug dealers, as criminals, and being dangerous. The existential tragedy of American culture is that there is a grain of truth in these stigmas for very practical reasons. How do young men and women having grown up in a community called *a cesspool of humanity*, or *a living nightmare* escape the stigma? How do we keep the stigma from being applied to everyone with dark skin? This is the very reason for the emergence of Critical Race Theory. If reasonable and compassionate people fully understand the history of race and the biology and neuroscience of how our minds work, we have a decent chance of mitigating racial bias. But given our tumultuous and hate-filled history, it is only a chance.

To be economically successful in life as a group requires generations of successful families. Few of us navigate our way to middle and upper-middle-class income levels without having had family assistance in some way, although assistance of this kind is so easily forgotten that it will often be denied by the individuals who have been helped the most. Many young people today are unaware that, in the 1950s, Black men and women were not just seen as being unqualified for jobs reserved for white people—they were often denied such opportunities by force, and some paid with crossing the traditional whites-only line with their lives. Nancy MacLean begins her book *Freedom is Not Enough: The Opening of the American Workplace,* with a story about a 37-year-old Black man who, upon being given a job normally reserved for whites in a Mississippi rubber plant, was murdered with a car bomb by fellow employees who were members of the Ku Klux Klan. His death was ruled an accident.[89] It took the Civil Rights Act of 1964 before there were any teeth in laws forbidding discrimination in the workplace based on race. In a chapter titled "The Rightness of Whiteness," MacLean says, "The culture of exclusion organized life in the United States in the early 1950s so thoroughly that it appeared natural and unremarkable to nearly all white Americans."[90] This socio-cultural reality occurred in my lifetime, and I remember the collective assumption accepted as common sense, precisely as she described it.

In the 1940s and 50s, resistance for African Americans entering the workforce as professionals was met with the same vitriol that Black children met when trying to enroll in all-white schools. I vividly recall colored restrooms and drinking fountains, So, no, after centuries of forced inequality, freedom of opportunity is not "get ready, get set, go" with everything from here forward being fair and fine. That life should be so simple and that people would have the nerve to call the centuries-old fight to rid the country of the lingering animus of systemic racial prejudice a *religion* is both contemptuous and shameful.

In her book *White Space, Black Hood: Opportunity Hoarding and Segregation in the Age of Inequality*, Sheryll Cashin refers to those trapped in high-poverty neighborhoods as 'descendants,' "in recognition of an unbroken continuum from slavery."[91] She writes:

> **Descendants are the group least likely in American society to experience the accoutrements of citizenship. Exit from the hood and from the bottom of the social order is improbable. Among the modern state action designed to contain descendants are militaristic policing in which Blackness itself becomes the pretext for stopping people, mass incarceration, the criminalization of poverty, a school-to-prison pipeline, and housing and school policies that invest in, rather than discourage, poverty concentration.**[92]

In *The 1619 Project* in a chapter titled "Progress," Ibram X. Kendi calls for a Third Reconstruction because of the failure of the Second.[93] In the Preface to the second paperback edition of *The Anatomy of Racial Inequality,* Glenn C. Loury argues that he would not want to take part in negotiations for reparations solely on behalf of African Americans. Instead, he writes, "Far better, in my view—more ethical and also more politically effective—would be to take our moral capital, combine it with the influence of others on behalf of creating of a decent social contract for all Americans, and work hard to get that implemented."[94]

Ironically, I agree with both Kendi and Loury. For reparations to become politically viable would require that the way our biology has handicapped our capacities for otherness would be experienced as common knowledge, enabling most people to fully understand the gravity of what centuries of overt racism has done to the lives of generations of African Americans. Racial animosity is being weaponized for political purposes, but open-mindedness about our history as peoples of the world could go a long way toward healing the current political divide. We desperately need a new Fairness Doctrine to address the purposeful misinformation that is tearing the country apart.

I believe that reparations for African Americans are, without a doubt, warranted, but the only viable political means of making it a reality, in my view, would be to improve life for poor whites as well, otherwise spite will become viral and politically weaponized. As I observed in *Blue Bias*, in 1967, the Johnson Administration conducted a study that made over 200 recommendations for making life better for all Americans, but especially those in America's inner cities.[95] Had these measures been taken, it is likely that current levels of racial inequality would be less severe. What needs to be understood today, though, by everyone concerned, is that the algorithmic nature of digital technology is threatening every level of employment in America because employees are being replaced by automation. This is especially applicable to America's inner cities which are still in need of serious investment.

Pulling all the above material together well enough to be able to explain the way our minds process bias to cause us to categorize people as the *other* is the only way I know how we might seriously put the brakes on the current cultural war, which is based on nothing but the dividends of racial animosity for political advantage. Achieving a critical mass of woke citizens in this country is a goal that, given where we are, seems to be impossible, but then, so did an end to slavery in 1850.

REFLECTIONS

One of the major impediments to finding common ground with those we have categorized as the *other* in any capacity is a pronounced inability to put oneself in the shoes of that person without feeling defensive. But this, in many cases, is not just an unwillingness to act: It appears that lots of people literally can't do it. My father, born in 1921, fit this description, and so did I, when I was young. I grew up in a hard-right political culture that was steeped in the notion of white superiority, and it took me years to unravel it. Research in neuroscience tells us that our anterior cingulate cortex, which is part of our limbic system, is at least partially the part of our brain that deals with empathy and emotional resolve.[96]

For people who cannot put themselves in the place of another without being defensive, the question we must ask, is this region of their brain simply underdeveloped from a lack of use? I suspect this may be the case, but currently I have no evidence to prove it. The very idea is so politically explosive that, in my view, it helps explain why it is not sufficiently addressed in educational theory. It is exceptionally hard to recall what it was like not to know something once we have learned it, but I still have an inkling of what it was like to have assumed that my cultural indoctrination was the one and only justifiable way to be in the world. Some people I believe are born with an exceptional ability to empathize and relate to others; for some it can be learned; and for some I suspect it is extremely difficult.

No one group, religion, occupation, race, creed, political party, club, or philosophy has a lock on virtue. None of us are so special that we are the only ones whose needs matter, yet this is precisely the view that so many undereducated citizens assume.

Having spent many years in an intensive effort of self-education, I don't have any trouble in putting myself in the shoes of others without becoming defensive. I can discuss white privilege, which I know is globally ubiquitous, without being offended or feeling defensive. To my thinking, the fact that so many of our citizens are either incapable of or unwilling to do this is, to a significant degree, why we are so politically divided.

Based only on my personal experience and speculation sparked by my research, I suspect that if one does not have a predilection for being able to see things from another's point of view, then being able to do so may depend upon having reached a critical mass of existential understanding as an educational tipping point so that one can apply perspective as an observer and not as an involved participant. This mode of understanding is to my thinking about as objective, in a humanitarian sense, as we can get.

I spent July through September of 2020 being interviewed about my book *Blue Bias*. As I have noted, the old-fashioned kind of racial prejudice still has an overt presence in policing. Indeed, the FBI has reported on the increasing number of white supremacists

infiltrating police departments.[97] So, as I have repeated ad nauseum, *overt* racism is not necessary to get a racist result: All that is
required is seeing another person who doesn't belong to our group
as being *different* so that we judge them with a nudge of cultural
influence based on the expectations of our life experience.

When you listen to a record album or CD with a long list of
songs over and over, when you get to the end of one, you may recall
the notes that are coming next before they play, without being
aware that you had remembered them—they just pop into your
mind. This analogy may be a bit of a stretch, but if we witness a race
or group of people characterized negatively in myriad instances
while growing up, then when occasions arise, we will recall "notes"
from these subconsciously observed experiences as intuitions. It is
highly likely that we will intuit that there was some validity in the
negative claims, even if minor or slight. Simply put, our brains are
paying attention when it seems we aren't, and appearances overwhelmingly trump what we think should be the case.

All over the world, misconceptions about how bias works
keep us from making progress in matters involving race relations.
Until most people fully understand how our brains work, we will
never make sufficient progress in race relations. We are never going
to solve the problem of implicit bias until we fully understand that
our brains strive to protect us from harm and embarrassment. In
centuries past, physical danger was common and frequent, but
embarrassment could also lead to death because of despotic cultural
authority. People were drawn and quartered simply from failing to
genuflect in respect to tyrants. If we have grown up in a country
in which racism is systemic, then, simply because of the way brains
process experience, it is impractical to expect that we will readily
admit making categorical assumptions without being aware that
we have done so if we don't fully understand this process. Trading

mental places with others to appreciate life from their point of view seems like such an underutilized method of finding common ground.

Every generation grows up internalizing their culture as it appears, and therefore, it can take centuries to alter biases and beliefs because significant changes happen slowly as each generation internalizes things as they seem. It has, for example, taken decades for the results of affirmative action to have made it crystal clear that equal opportunity was always warranted because Black people are just as talented as white people. If you are old enough, this won't require further explanation because you were there in the culture that expressed serious doubts that Black people could qualify for professional employment. This wasn't that long ago; it was the time of colored drinking fountains and separate bathrooms. The haunting question is why our behavioral professionals have not yet explained to the public how racial bias is passed from one generation to the next, but the answer is decidedly simple: Most have not yet figured it out. They have not clarified the dynamics of implicit bias because so many still apparently believe that this is a subject we can handle through the consciousness of our frontal cortex, without acknowledging the profound influence that our subconscious has on our states of mind. It is imperative to understand that, in making instantaneous caution-based decisions, our brains are functioning as designed, in that we are wired with a sentinel limbic system still attuned to the dangers of the Stone Age, which makes us intuitively wary of strangers, change and uncertainty. This pronounced result of evolution *must* be considered common knowledge before we can mitigate hidden prejudice.

It is difficult to overstate the fact that racial animosity and hatred are not necessary to produce incidents with a racist result. All that it takes is subconsciously seeing someone as "not one of us." This is more than enough to put a finger on the scales and treat a stranger just a little bit differently than those with whom we are more comfortable. If the person is of a different race, it increases the likelihood that we have previously categorized them as being different from our group. For police officers, this minute difference in categorization can make the difference in shoot/don't shoot. All that is necessary in a shoot/don't shoot scenario is to perceive, in milliseconds, that this person in front of you represents the *other* in any sense, to *any* degree. Moreover, many other factors are in play in these situations: the neighborhood, race, gender, if is at night, if one is already stressed, mood, even temperature.

We are never going to deal effectively with the subject of racial bias in this country until we face up to the fact that our brains work the way they evolved to work, not as we wish them to work. Once we realize that we are predisposed to be hyperaware of all reasons for caution and suspicion where otherness is involved, we can set about to think our way through the matters at hand and mitigate the effects of implicit bias. Until then, nothing much is likely to mitigate unconscious bias.

And thus, we continuously experience a perpetual conflict between our conscious and subconscious minds. The great tragedy here is that this remains an open secret, because, unfortunately, most people in America still believe that their conscious mind is completely in charge here, and if they feel no racial animosity: case closed. Simply put, brains cause bias and the conflict between our subconscious and conscious minds confuses us. It is like having a friend that tells us something important, then denies having said it. Awareness is necessary to pierce cognitive confusion.

Racial animosity has a chameleon, viral-like quality that frequently changes size, shape, tenor, and tone, but whose shadowy presence always awaits the heat of emotion to make itself known.

CONCERNED CITIZENS

If your reason for having read this far in this book is because you are a concerned citizen who wishes to learn about the nature of bias, then you are way out front in the effort to mitigate implicit racial bias. Regardless of your occupation or your reasons for being interested in this subject, you already have the most important motivation by far, in that you *care*. As I hope I have made clear, the importance of caring can't be overemphasized. A first step is for everyone to admit that there is a problem of bias in this country. Given the evidence, this should be a lot easier than it is. Your level of knowledge and concern can be critical to your life and career and can negatively or positively affect the lives of others. If this is the case, your study and scholarship in the behavioral sciences should be continuous and lifelong.

If your occupation or life circumstances entail that you will frequently encounter situations that call for your judgment in matters where bias is known to have a negative history of overt prejudice, then you need to realize that your education in this regard has only just started. If the subject of bias is of personal importance to you, then you need to realize that the development of science about the nature of human bias is still in its infancy. Follow the science: Seek out the behavioral professionals on the cutting edge of human biology and neuroscience. For example, much of what has been learned about the hormone oxytocin (often called the love hormone) is recent. It has only been in the last couple of decades that scientists have learned that, at a certain tipping point, oxytocin is also instrumental in a predilection to ostracize and otherize others, so to speak.[98] The only thing that can keep you from being an expert on the subject of bias is a lack of interest. If you are truly interested, it won't take that long to become familiar with most of what has been learned about this subject.

If your interest in this subject is only one of curiosity and you are not able to make decisions that affect the lives of others when it comes to bias, you can still contribute by understanding the subject of bias well enough to explain it to others. Take the Implicit Association Test (IAT) at Harvard University. It is online and open to anyone.[99] The IAT measures the reaction time it takes when we are asked questions about race with the assumption that a longer pause suggests that the subject one is looking at has a greater chance of being considered the other. The argument about the reliability of the IAT is long and heated, and it is far from settled. But in my view, it is worth the effort, even if you can't fully reconcile the results to your own satisfaction, because the thought process itself is insightful. Its effectiveness at discerning bias on an individual level may be questionable, but in the aggregate, when revealing the bias at a group level, the test does seem more effective. It is really a simple process. If it takes us longer to react to a face—in other words, if we are unfamiliar with the unfamiliarity—it suggests a distancing. In other words, if we must stop and think about the race of the person we are looking at when being asked to make a judgment and we can't decide on the spot, then it suggests to me that there is little doubt that we are viewing this person as not being one of us. That the context of how and where and in what mood we are in may give different results when taking the test multiple times is easy to understand when you examine how much context and *noise* matters in human behavior. You have nothing to lose but your naïveté, so take the test and study the pro and con arguments about its validity. If one concerned citizen uses this work to help eliminate their own racial bias, this effort will have been worth it.

Recall that earlier I described our tribalistic behavior as being analogous to having a chemical factory in our heads. In 2012, researchers at the Oxford University Centre for Neuroethics discovered that the beta blocker propranolol (a blood pressure drug) has the effect of abolishing implicit bias. They made this discovery by measuring the results of Harvard's IAT test-takers' responses after they were given the drug.[100] This is a fascinating discovery. Does this mean we can use pills to eliminate racism? It is not that simple, of course, but hopefully this finding will result in vigorous research about how hormones affect our behavior and our understanding of the chemical nature of racial biases.

In his book *Behave*, endocrinologist Robert M. Sapolsky makes the point repeatedly that human biology is complicated. The truly exciting thing, to my thinking, is that when it comes to learning about the chemical processes taking place in our heads, much of what we know is barely three decades old. This research is still in its infancy. History suggests that we are likely to learn things about our biological nature that in time prove to be wrong, but the major criteria, in my view, to fight the negative effects of implicit racial bias, are in the collective will to care deeply about doing so. It is easy, for example, to imagine the pharmaceutical industry going off the rails by promising to end racism with medication. The efficacy of such an approach could easily become misused and corruptible. We can't, however, fix what we don't know about, and history shows that we don't fix what we don't care about.

POLICE OFFICERS

As a police officer, you are on the frontlines of efforts to help mitigate racial bias. Your attention to day-to-day actions regarding race always have the potential to make headline news, so much so that a significant amount of time without an incident would itself be treated as news.

There have been great changes in technology since I was a Dallas police officer in the 1960s, and some tactical changes, but the interactions between the police and the public haven't changed at all. I know from personal experience and years of scholarship that whether you are a rookie or a seasoned veteran, regardless of your ethnicity, if you haven't studied the history of policing and race in depth, then you are insufficiently grounded in fully understanding what your presence as an officer of the law means to the people you are sworn to protect. *Protect* is the operative word here. I know what it is like to work shift after shift in poverty-stricken *high-crime* neighborhoods that I refer to in *Blue Bias* as cortisol canyons—communities where squad cars cruising one after another down dark unlit streets at night often resemble predators looking for prey.

In my view, having given this more than a half century's thought, the key to community policing in traditionally impoverished communities must be public safety above and beyond the number of misdemeanor arrests, traffic tickets, and court summons. Citizens in these neighborhoods must feel safe from bad actors and police harassment before there is any possibility for trusting the police enough to enlist strong public support. Police departments that judge their effectiveness solely on numerical indices misjudge their ability to achieve their objective to *protect and serve*. Your police rank may severely limit your ability to have any positive effect on this, but understanding the importance of the public's need to feel safe over all other measures is critical to effective policing. Make no mistake: The citizens in cortisol canyons want criminals arrested. What they don't want is to feel like perpetual suspects because of where they live and what they look like. In most neighborhoods where you work, if you have been there long, you are likely to know the identity of the repeat offenders and they deserve your attention, but overly aggressive policing that treats everyone as a potential offender with incessant traffic stops and the frequent interrogation of citizens just walking in their neighborhoods is less effective in preventing crime than it is in upping the stress level of the people who live there. Moreover, if you aren't busy during quiet periods looking for petty offenses, then you will be available during real emergencies when the people you serve really need your help.

Again, your rank may prevent you from influencing your department's policy regarding community policing, but if you learn enough about the history of policing and race, you can convince others about the importance of public safety in every community. And who knows? You may be chief someday. If you truly live up to your oath to protect and serve, and heed the lessons about how bias works, you will be instrumental in setting an example worth emulating and we likely won't be watching your career implode in a YouTube video. If one police officer uses this text to improve their policing, then this will have been worth it. One final reminder: As a police officer and as a citizen, you have the right to your own political opinion, but politics has no business with your presence on the street where you work.

Unfortunately, policing attracts people with authoritarian personalities, people who view the world in rigid, black-and-white terms, whose approach to law enforcement is extreme intolerance, over-aggression, and often excessive mean-spiritedness. If you are a seasoned veteran of law enforcement, you are bound to know individuals who meet this criterion in matters of degree. If justice is to be blind, then to be just, authoritarianism as a policy has no place in law enforcement. Authoritarianism is an ideology that feeds on its own success in that it ratchets up and increases its routine authority in the severity of its methods of operation. There is no room in an open society for an ideology that fosters continuous animosity toward social groups that it doesn't understand or approve of if they are breaking no laws. This kind of environment is antithetical to the ethos to protect and serve.

TEACHERS

In his book, *Why Teach: In Defense of Real Education,* Mark Edmundson said:

> The quest at the center of a liberal arts education is not a luxury quest; it's a necessity quest. If you do not undertake it, you risk a life of desperation—maybe quiet; maybe, in time, very loud—and I am not exaggerating. For you risk trying to be someone other than who you are, which in the long run, is killing.[101]

I am not exaggerating when I say that, for people who are fundamentally unaware of how our brains work in processing our life experience, that if the way our minds work can't become common knowledge, then we are doomed to continue repeating the mindless finger-pointing about whether one is a racist or not, all the while missing the point. It is so critically important that this endeavor is successful in recruiting teachers. Teachers are the point of the spear of education in this country. The advice in this book is not Critical Race Theory. This is simply human biology applied to race and socialization. Going through life without fully understanding how our minds direct our attention is like having a GPS that is a few miles out of kilter.

My generation was taught that stereotypes are bad, so it became routine for us to deny having them. Stereotyping is simply our brain's method of flagging our reality map as we go through life's journey to make it possible to keep going without getting lost, and to stay safe if we ever come this way again. Our stereotyping helps us to navigate. Now, once we learn that these shortcuts for decision-making were made involuntarily, without our conscious awareness, there may be a temptation to suggest that because this is the case, then we aren't responsible for our biases. But the quest for a liberal education is likely to encounter arguments like this one from Henry David Thoreau, who argued that if we are the beneficiaries of an unjust society, then we are personally responsible for making it just.

Hopefully teachers will accept the challenge to stop the nonsensical arguments about whether one is a racist based on one's conscious feelings and be able to successfully explain how our minds categorize, stereotype, and stigmatize. While we are not responsible for how our brains have accomplished this while we are growing up, if we can be made aware that what we have internalized is harmful to others, we have a responsibility to make it right. Getting this across to people whose minds are made up that, because they have no ill feelings toward others means they simply don't have any bias, is an extraordinary existential challenge, but the goodwill and wellbeing of the country is dependent upon getting this done.

In his book, *Teaching for Critical Thinking: Tools and Techniques to Help Students Question Their Assumptions*, Stephen

D. Brookfield describes how important it has been to tell students that he himself struggles at times with difficult material but that with perseverance and determination it will all fall into place.

In 1899, psychologist William James published *Talks to Teachers on Psychology and to Students on Some of Life's Ideals.* He said one general aphorism ought to dominate conduct in the classroom. "*No reception without reaction, no impression without correlative expression,*—this is the great maxim which the teacher ought never to forget." He added that, "Any impression which simply flows in at the pupil's eyes or ears, and in no way modifies his active life, is an impression gone to waste. It is physiologically incomplete."[102] Indeed, this especially applies to both children and adults when the subject is bias. One needs to be able to acknowledge that a problem exists and be able to relate to the concerns of those negatively affected before any sense of personal responsibility can take hold.

The late Neil Postman was an extraordinary teacher. He wrote twenty books about his craft, and he argued persuasively that education should be thought of as "a defense against culture."[103] He said that over three decades ago. A few years later, he called attention to the United States as being not really a culture so much as just being an economy and the "last refuge of an exhausted philosophy of education."[104] Postman said that, in "most places school is conceived of as a form of indoctrination, the continuation of politics by gentle means."[105] If he were here today, I can imagine what he would have to say about historically undereducated parents raging against the teaching of the history of racism. Postman observed that all the knowledge we have is the result of questions, yet we don't teach the art of questioning as a major educational objective.[106]

Today's political polarization is such that education as a defense against culture applies as a grossly understated objective.

Education today may be the last chance we have to survive as a Democratic Republic. Teachers can lead the way by helping dissipate hatred and contempt born of ignorance by simply teaching critical brain theory. The existence and exponential growth of social media and echo-chamber news organizations that run on vitriol and contempt are tearing the country apart by feeding our tribalistic fears and hyping our worst instincts. It is worth repeating that we desperately need a new 21st Century Fairness Doctrine to help decrease political animus. Propagandist-driven fake news is a major force in political polarization, and it is hard to control because it feeds on itself.

At the core of my philosophy of self-education is my conviction that an education should be thought of not as something you get, but as something you take. This is not a posture of contempt for traditional education, nor is it an attitude of belligerence toward the teaching profession. What it amounts to, if you really think it through, is a psychological paradigm shift of Emersonian proportions. Thinking of an education as something you take, as naturally as your next breath, is the heart of Emerson's notion of self-reliance.

I've been writing books and essays about the value of self-education for more than 35 years, and my life experience suggests that Abraham Maslow should have included the need for learning in his Hierarchy of Needs Theory. Early on in formal education, every child should be made aware of the formula for self-reinforcing learning, which is simply that if we try to learn about most any subject, the degree to which we achieve a critical mass of knowledge—a point where adding new information causes a kaleidoscopic cerebral reorganization, resulting in an endorphin rush—then learning will become its own self-perpetuating reward system.

This is the impetus that makes hobbies habitually rewarding activities, yet this remains an open secret. It makes me wonder why we don't make a big deal about making sure everyone knows how this process works. The criteria may indeed be a little different for everyone, but the formula is pretty much the same. From ants to aerospace, the world is full of enthralling subjects.

For generations academics have routinely discovered the self-reinforcing rewards of intensive learning. Many have built their lives on the experience, and they devote their lives to trying to pass it on, but seldom do they ever do so by explaining how the process that makes learning so intrinsically rewarding works. This is a case where "telling" might work even better than "showing" for some of us, because if one stops short of achieving a critical mass of knowledge, the endorphin reward experience doesn't occur. There is also the added benefit in becoming the go-to person in any subject arena because it offers an increase in social status. So, the reward from learning via an endorphin rush is also attenuated by a reputation for having achieved a level of expertise which is easily interpreted as being an admirable person.

So, imagine, you go to school one day and tell your students, "Listen up, children, I'm going to give you the secret to a fulfilling and purposeful life. All you need to do is find something that you truly care about, something you find exceptionally interesting, then build on it, until adding knowledge becomes a reward of its own right, and your expertise in the subject matter begins to validate your feelings of existence as a valuable citizen. Got it? No worries, if it's not clear at this point, we will work on it."

WHAT CAN YOU DO?

- Study the history of racial bias.
- Follow authors who are engaged in eliminating bias.
- Follow research in behavioral sciences.
- Follow research in biology and neuroscience.
- Put regularly scheduled keyword searches into Google.
- List the categorizations you are likely to encounter.
- List the stigmas you are likely to encounter.
- Practice shifting thinking from System One to Two.
- Take the IAT.
- Contemplate your IAT test results.
- If you identified *others,* spend time with them.
- Listen to opposing views.
- Identify what you consider your core values.
- Practice putting yourself in the *other's* shoes.
- Engage in *civil* dialogue about race.
- Facilitate discussions.
- Evaluate your discussions.

- Realize that authoritarianism is the seedbed of hatred.
- Critique the criminal justice system on race.
- Explain to others what you have learned.
- Critique racially charged YouTube videos.
- Read the views of those you oppose.
- Critique the culture you grew up in for implicit and explicit bias.
- Realize critical thinking requires deconstructing assumptions.
- Realize some things are too obvious to see clearly.
- Pay attention to local politics.
- Vote thoughtfully.
- Write your elected representatives.
- Realize debunking categorization and stigma require significant effort.
- Read, read, read.

EPILOGUE

Extrinsic racial bias, or the old-fashioned kind of hate, has resurfaced so forcefully that it's comparable to a cold civil war, so much so that it gives a new meaning to the term *social distancing*. Hate crimes are skyrocketing, school boards are banning books, and, in some states, teachers are forbidden to even discuss issues about race and gender. Efforts to forbid books and lessons about race and gender are antithetical to civilization. They forcibly shut down System Two thinking and depend upon System One (automatic pilot), which is the driving force of unconscious biases. It should be clear by now, that, if our brains work as they have evolved to do, we become very picky about people we don't know and circumstances that are unfamiliar. Silencing the desperately needed dialogue to mitigate our tribalistic differences is a recipe for social animosity. We can't fix what we don't understand or talk about.

In some communities, citizens who have no idea what it truly represents are both manic and frantic about Critical Race Theory. I don't know how to solve this problem and unfortunately our history offers very little help. But I do have faith that, when it comes to the surreptitious influence of our subconscious biases, concerned citizens can make a big difference by overwriting these Stone Age predilections. Cultures shelter us from reality, and they also serve as theaters of desire and aspirations as we learn while we are growing up to want what others want. What others think and what they believe is far, far, more important to us than we are traditionally taught to believe. When in the company of others, when we speak, we are often, for myriad reasons, extraordinarily careful about what we say. Geographically, we even mimic our fellow citizens by talking like they do. Thus, our relations with others and our cultural expectations have a profound influence on our behavior and the way we see the world.

There is a tendency when we turn to biology and neuroscience to assume that since we are wired for tribalistic behavior that nothing more can or should be done. Yes, we have brains whetted during prehistory, but we are living in a technological age bordering on magic. Moreover, to flourish in a Democratic Republic requires an intellectual buy-in, along with the knowledge and vigilance necessary to make self-government viable. Our social relations with one another as Americans are critical to our success. A system based on democracy and the better argument demands that Americans identify as one tribe, and that racism is experienced as a "corrupted norm."[107] Given that some of our Stone Age predilections no longer serve us well, it is critical that we realize that we are already biologically equipped with the ability to overwrite our biased unconscious assumptions. When we understand what we are up against, we are well prepared to mitigate implicit biases once we are fully aware of their existence. We need to question so many of the things we have always taken for granted.

The Dawn of Everything: A New History of Humanity by David Graeber and Davis Wengrow is an exciting and exhilarating work, raising far more questions than it answers as it challenges myriad dogmatic assumptions about prehistory.[108] These authors pose questions about the past that call for a serious rethinking of some of our typical stereotypes of our ancestors and, in doing so, they expose the way the word *primitive* is so often used with pejorative bias, driven in no small part by contemporary arrogance. These authors aspire to restore our ancestors to their full humanity by revealing archaeological evidence that contradicts so much of what was assumed to be far less sophisticated than it had to be simply to survive.

This book strikes an existential chord with me because my goal is similar. Our species evolved with a subtle but sentinel awareness that is currently undermining American civility. Our full measure of humanity comes with the biological and intellectual capability for overcoming our propensity to judge others based on our subconscious take on reality. A reappraisal of the past calls for a much closer examination of the present.

The spirit of *The Dawn of Everything* makes me reflective about using the word inevitable in the title of this book. I have thought about this point at great length, and I can't come up with a better explanation for the ubiquity of racial prejudice—nothing better than the biological fact that we are wired this way for simple but profound reasons about survival. I have had people take exception to the possibility that our biology made racism inevitable. In my view, the evidence that our very subtle but hypersensitive sentinel awareness for danger in all its many manifestations is overwhelmingly the cause of implicit bias hopefully by now is self-evident. The ubiquitous presence of racial bias is to a significant degree default behavior. Encountering situations that traditionally involve biases simply calls for shifting our thinking gears from System One to System Two when circumstances warrant it.

One method to help develop this skill is one used by therapists to help treat a variety of mental health concerns. Cognitive Behavioral Therapy (CBT) is about reframing and rethinking our approach to dealing with our subconscious, and may be a useful tool to employ when working to shift those gears.[109] Detailed research about CBT's effects on mitigating implicit bias has yet to be done, but its past success in aiding people to "reprogram" negative and unproductive ways of thinking has potential in this field.

It is a grave error to dismiss the influence of our subconscious, assuming that our frontal cortex is the sole source of our awareness and motivation. Just as if we have had the chicken pox when we were children, the shingles virus is in our bodies—if we have grown up in a culture where racial bias is a normative reality, then we are likely to have internalized implicit biases that lay dormant like the shingles, until occasions that call for them to surface. The only viable way to control this kind of behavioral influence is to be hyperaware of how this biological process works and to apply executive or frontal cortex thinking when occasions call for it.

Restoring our species to our full humanity will rightfully acknowledge that we are also equipped with the gray matter that can temper the negative effects of our biological wariness. We must simply be able to recognize the occasions when we need to metaphorically patch our software by applying executive-level thinking to overcome and overwrite our culturally biased subconscious assumptions. It is in the complex nature of racial relations that for this subject, there can never be a last word: There is always more to consider, more to say, more to explain.

The authors of *The Dawn of Everything* remind us that we define ourselves by our differences with others.[110] By now it should be clear that we are supersensitive about our differences with others, that we are subconsciously aware, even when it appears we aren't paying attention. Minor differences matter. They matter a lot. In *Civilization and its Discontents*, Sigmund Freud called our attention to the fact that where countries border one another, the significance of minor differences are often sensationally dramatized.[111] He ended this piece in 1930, wondering how and to what extent our species might be able to compensate for our antiquated instincts, which applies perfectly to overcoming racial biases today. Saying that our kind is identity crazed is not a stretch. Differences are how we identify the *other*. Our sense of identity trumps many of our natural fears, which helps explain why millions of Americans fear an attack on their political identity more than they fear dying from COVID-19.

We are extremely fond of similarities, yet our differences give us leverage, an edge, so to speak. Children will pester and bully children whose differences are noticeable, but when we compete with others who want what we want, it is our differences with others that help us make our case that we are better suited or qualified. My point in this explanation is to demonstrate how difficult it is to ignore the influence others have on our worldviews. The reason we are so heavily influenced by cultural prejudice is because what our fellow citizens think and believe is vitally important to us. As Todd Rose explains in his book, *Collective Illusions,* our desire to fit in and belong is so powerful that we are profoundly influenced by what we assume others think. We are unlikely to disregard what we believe is accepted public opinion. If most everyone seems to hold prejudices about race and gender, it is highly unlikely that we will fail to give them credence. We often fall for collective illusions based on mistaken assumptions about what others are thinking. Rose argues that we share deep biological yearnings to identify with the majority.[112] It is illogical to expect that the racial animosity my generation grew up experiencing in the South in the 1940s and 50s was something that we could have denied, ignored, or dismissed, or that it could even be dealt with effectively today without a concentrated effort to do so.

Our respective cultures are rife with expectations about how we are to behave. When we perceive acts of discrimination based on race as we are growing up, we don't think, "I am not going to give this observation any credence because I don't believe it is right." We just record the experience subconsciously because our need to fit in and to belong is profoundly important to us, whether we consciously acknowledge it or not. Human brains can be characterized as prediction machines.[113] Think about it this way: We could not be surprised if we had not already incurred a baseline of assumptions. We are surprised when circumstances don't match our biases. If, for example, we see a poorly dressed Black man, only to learn he is a famous neurosurgeon, what would this tell us?

The case simply cannot be overstated: There are no good reasons to hate people because of their race. That a political party would use race as a fear-based political tactic is unworthy of public support in a democratic republic. A culture war about race in America is cancerous—it is a losing proposition on all sides. Outlawing the study of controversial subjects is an anathema to an open society. We are an imperfect species and we have evolved to favor our own kind. Racial prejudice is not rocket science, but it is just as important, if not much more so. It is critical to fully understand and enthusiastically appreciate the time-worn reality, that, just because we suddenly perceive that we see the light and declare that all forms of racial bias are wrong, the problem is still not solved. The subconscious assumptions that we have spent our lives recording beneath our conscious awareness are still there, and they are there to stay.[114] We still don't know how to completely overwrite them. The next time we encounter a situation in which an opinion about race is called for, if we are not hyperaware, the old influence will light back up. Subconscious assumptions based on years of lived experience in a culture in which racial bias is systematic are analogous to smoldering coals in a slightly dormant fire—all it takes is a little puff of wind to reignite, flare up, and burn brightly. Racial animosity sleeps, but it never dies.

The number of people in this country who believe themselves exempt from harboring any vestige of racial bias is astounding when we compare the data and statistics that show the pervasiveness of implicit and explicit prejudice in America. Millions of well-meaning people in this country are resolutely certain that, since they feel no racial animosity when making decisions in which opinions are called for about race, they maintain no bias. Therefore, the mindless, senseless arguments about whether one is a racist or not never get us anywhere. I will argue vigorously that many of the decisions that result in a racist result had no ill will intended; they are instead likely the influence of subconscious assumptions that appear in the form of an intuitive nudge based on a lifetime of being immersed in a culture that has assumed its version of reality based on inferences, appearances, and messy popular-opinion perceptions. This is how human resource personnel who do the hiring interviews can consider themselves bias free and enthusiastically progressive, while the data about their hiring decisions show a clear racial bias. This applies to police arrests, traffic stops, judges' sentencing in criminal trials, credit applications…and the list goes on, through every situation in society in which the potential for racial bias exists. If we swim in water in which a toxic chemical is present, we will likely have been contaminated, however slightly. The same holds for having grown up in a society where racial discrimination is ubiquitous: Escaping without having been influenced enough to put a light finger on the scales in judgment calls is damned near impossible.

In a rational society, being woke, as in fully understanding how human brains store, foster, and fester myriad biases, would be considered a noble aspiration. There would be no need to make fun of those who have striven to learn how this Stone Age cerebral process evolved to help our ancestors survive in a dangerous world. The fact that we grow up without gaining a reasonable appreciation of how our minds work with relation to bias and belief is crippling, both politically and in terms of our psychological equilibrium. We tilt in favor of being human doings instead of human beings. In other words, our actions make our lives more confusing than they might be if we simply knew why we believe and act as we do, because of the contextual circumstances we experience.

It's sort of analogous to being mystified by shadows without understanding the effects of the sun. We literally have enough research about how our minds work that we could prepare a novice owner's manual for our species, yet it would be much less prescriptive than simply a perpetual warning to be cautious, so as not to mistake what we see when we look out upon the world as straight-up reality.

That our gray matter is obsessed 24/7 to peg reality beneath our conscious awareness to keep us safe from harm and embarrassment and that this process is prone to cataloging mistaken assumptions that subvert our social relations is very clear, and that this sentinel awareness served us better during prehistory than today is becoming more and more obvious every year. That we need a patch in the form of an existential education to help dissipate the festering animosity, due to mistaking shadows for reality, is also critical for the creation of a viable future. Simply put, we have the technology of wizards, while too many of our citizens have mindsets more suitable for the Stone Age than today.

Another way to grasp how our biological nature negatively affects our social relations with others is to appreciate what happens if we are developmentally impaired. Williams Syndrome (WMS) is a genetic disorder that enhances language abilities while rendering the person overly friendly and trusting to the point of being exceptionally easily to manipulate.[115] A society where everyone trusted each other would likely have been short-lived. If we don't acknowledge that we need to update our Stone Age predilections to compensate for our biases which cause us to default to acting anti-social and inappropriate simply because we are being influenced by what we assume other people think, then ours too may be short-lived. But in order to combat our predispositions to bias, we must first conquer that which stands in our way: indifference.

In *The Rapture of Maturity*, I argued that mainstream indifference is a form of ignorance born of inattention and apathy. Depending solely upon appearances, it is fed by pettiness and a gravitation toward whatever seems easiest. It revels in anti-aesthetics, un-mindfulness, bad faith, and a total lack of reflection about matters vital for making sense of the world. These are not half-hearted but half-headed efforts. Mainstream indifference is devoid of compassion; it is a hostile, authoritarian, and testosterone-laden environment where the weak are ridiculed and the poor are held in contempt regardless of the circumstances for their plight.

In effect, mainstream indifference is a selfish, cliché-ridden, and narrow-minded refuge for racists, bigots, misanthropes, and misogynists. It's a psychological wasteland where thoughtless people are bound together by a yoke of stupidity which is wholly accepted as plain old common sense. However, such thinking frequently betrays itself through seething hatred, complete with public demonstrations of contempt for "others." A lack of curiosity is the real culprit. This social realm is anti-intellectual to the

101

bone, feeding upon a disdain for eloquence in literature, the arts, and all serious endeavors that require cerebral verve. This deeply internalized conviction is often vested in superstition, intermingled with conspiracy theory, and held so dear that it cannot be acknowledged for what it really is—a profoundly malignant strain of despair shared by a fearful populace who are unified by their own lack of awareness and bonded by a form of hatred so spurious that it feeds off of itself. I understand this level of relating to society because I was a frequent participant before I began my own journey of self-education. I have seen how such insensitivity can infect otherwise good people who haven't set out to harm others but wind up doing so because of an inherent default to the worst human instincts. Indifference lies at its core.

One last time, at risk of ad nauseum, think about it this way—throughout our lives, beginning to end, we pay attention to what is going on in the world without being consciously aware we are doing so. In a nutshell, our species subconsciously records popular culture as representing social reality. We do this because we care deeply about what our fellow citizens think. Even if we strongly disagree, we are still likely to be influenced by public opinion because we are social creatures. Arguing incessantly that, since we feel no racial animosity toward others, we can't possibly make judgments that reflects cultural biases is to be willfully blind to the overwhelming evidence to the contrary.

All you must do to realize that you have internalized the essence of the culture you have grown up about race in America is to ask yourself if it is better to be white than black in this country. If you know this to be true, then rest assured, deep down, your limbic system worked precisely as it evolved to do. It means even if you don't agree, you won't need any explanation about why, for example, the British Royal Family were concerned about how dark

Prince Harry and Meghan's child might be. We need to acknowledge our affection for similarities and our predilections toward intolerance and apply what we have learned to compensate. Our future depends on it.

Authoritarian ideologies are a growing global concern. In America, we are in danger of democracy becoming the *New Lost Cause*. The list is long, and obstruction of justice is only the most glaring offense. But to put this concern in perspective, the Black Lives Matter Movement's grievance about longing for social justice began with America's beginning, and it has never been finally achieved and fulfilled with confidence that it will continue as our laws decree. It is long past time that we acknowledge how our minds work by applying biology, neuroscience, and evolutionary psychology to the subject of racial prejudice. The evidence is overwhelming that, for centuries, the ubiquity of implicit racial bias is because our brains have been working as designed. We need to bring our full humanity forward by thoughtfully overwriting this predilection. Concerned citizens, police officers and teachers, we need your help. Please review the annotated reading list that follows and help spread the word that in less than a couple hours of reading, you can help change the world.

ANNOTATED
SUGGESTED READING

If you really want to learn about the dynamics of how our human minds work and remain on the cutting edge of such knowledge well enough to readily explain it to others, my recommendation is to read all the books on this list and add to it as your interests grow. Neuroscience is beginning to explain what has from the beginning been considered unexplainable about human behavior. Over the next half century, this discipline will undoubtedly add to our understanding about what is so hard about getting along with people who simply see things differently than we do. Right now, shedding light on the dynamics of bias and getting beyond the senseless arguments about race is imperative if we are going to survive as a viable Republic.

The New Jim Crow: Mass Incarceration in the Age of
  Colorblindness, by Michelle Alexander.

  This book is Michelle Alexander's effort to start a conversation about how mass incarceration has effectively replaced the Jim Crow-era laws that have oppressed African Americans in this country since post-Reconstruction, and with thousands of reviews on Amazon, she has been successful. This book has had lots of criticism precisely because her documented research strikes many nerves. Here are some of her comments about the war on drugs: "The impact of the drug war has been astounding. In less than thirty years, the U.S. penal population exploded from around 300,000 to more than 2 million, with drug convictions accounting for the majority of the increase.... The racial dimension of mass incarceration is its most striking feature."[116] See the endnotes for a link to an interview of Michelle Alexander discussing *The New Jim Crow*.[117]

The Nature of Prejudice, by Gordon W. Allport.

This book is a classic, a timeless examination of the nature of prejudice. Some of Allport's techniques are as applicable as if this book had been published today. In this 500-plus page tome, you will find 31 chapters about nearly every aspect of prejudice one can consider, from definitions, to the normality of prejudgment and the functionality of in-group/out-group psychology. If only Allport had had the availability of today's tools of neuroscience, I suspect the subject of racial bias would be much better understood today.

Rise of the Warrior Cop: The Militarization of America's Police Forces, by Radley Balko.

Radley Balko shows how the militarization of policing in America has reached levels most of us never expected. Like me, he argues that his book is not anticop, but with so much politicization today, it is a challenge to offer any constructive criticism without being accused of hating cops. He says, if anything, his book is anti-politician, and I can relate to that as well. Balko warns that we aren't in a police state yet, but we are headed in that direction, and he shows in detail how this plays out from post-Reconstruction to today. Balko compares modern policing with the Praetorian Guard of ancient Rome and the parallels call to attention how easily police power becomes a tool of executive power.

Blindspot: ***Hidden Biases of Good People***, by Mahzarin R. Banaji and Anthony G. Greenwald.

This is an excellent treatise on the severe limitations of human rationality. These two psychologists have a lot to say about the Harvard IAT, about what it actually implies if one shows a white preference, for example. They argue, and I agree, that this is not proof of racial hostility; what it suggests to me is that it demonstrates that those who are not white are viewed as having been categorized simply as not one of us. Thus my take is that stigmatization will be easier as a result. They examine stereotypes, categories, and the perceptual illusions we encounter, which they call mindbugs. Highly recommended.

Us and Them: Understanding Your Tribal Mind, by David Berreby.

In my view, this is the best book in print about the subject of identity. Here Berreby writes, "Today, perhaps for the first time in human history, large masses of people recognize that human kinds are made, not discovered, Globalization is showing people that *our side* is determined by beliefs, not facts. It's now obvious that human-kind violence belongs to no one religion, nation, race, culture, or political ideology; it's equally obvious that a *good man* at home can be a torturer at work and that supposedly ancient hatreds can disappear, even as supposedly peaceful societies can turn genocidal. All of this has led to a hunger for new ways to think about human kinds."[118] See the endnotes for a link to David Berreby discussing his work on YouTube.[119]

Teaching for Critical Thinking: Tools and Techniques to Help Students Question Their Assumptions, by Stephen D. Brookfield.

This book covers a subject critical to civic functionality, with a conversational style that is easy to understand and apply when understanding difficult material is the objective. Brookfield's methods of examining fundamental assumptions that we grow up without questioning are a fundamental requirement for critical thinking.

Lynching in the New South: Georgia and Virginia 1880-1930, by W. Fitzhugh Brundage.

This book examines 600 lynchings over a half century in Georgia and Virginia. Reading this text, it is hard not to lose oneself in imagining what it must have been like for African Americans during these years. That this is not common knowledge helps explain the persistence of racial prejudice today.

Chokehold: Policing Black Men, by Paul Butler.

A book that carefully describes the double standard in policing and the criminal justice system. Based on my personal experience, I can't refute anything Professor Butler has written in *Chokehold.* Butler is a former prosecutor who has sent lots of Black men to prison, with regrets about having done so in some cases. Butler cites statistics that Black police officers are harder on Black people than white officers. When one understands the nature of racial bias, this makes sense. He also cites studies that show that the darker a Black man is, the more harshly he is likely to be treated by the criminal justice system. He also writes about the negative effects of stop and frisk. Paul Butler makes the point clear that the Civil Rights Movement in America didn't improve things for African Americans nearly as much as is commonly thought.

White Space, Black Hood: Opportunity Hoarding and
Segregation in the Age of Inequality, by Sheryll Cashin.

Cashin traces the history of government-created ghettos in Baltimore, St. Louis, Chicago, New York, and Cleveland. She shows that living in the hood is stressful to the point of being life-shortening and that until we deal with this egregious social disparity, historical inequality will continue unabated.

The Matter of Black Lives, edited by Jelani Cobb and
David Remnick.

This is a collection of groundbreaking essays by *The New Yorker* featuring the works of James Baldwin, Toni Morrison, Ta-Nehisi Coates, Henry Louis Gates, Jr., Malcom Gladwell and others who offer a sweeping portrait of Black Life in America.

White Fragility: Why It's So Hard for White People to Talk About Race, and *Nice Racism: How Progressive White People Perpetuate Racial Harm*, by Robin DiAngelo.

There is a lot of discussion, some from African Americans, about the viability of white people making a case about racism because they can never fully experience the feelings of being the target of such prejudice. I have been interested in this subject for more than fifty years and I have never run across a white person whose knowledge of the dynamics of racism is as deep and insightful as Robin DiAngelo's work. I can think of no nuanced social conflict about race that she hasn't dealt with using insight and compassion. Her books are worth multiple readings. Here are comments from the Introduction of *White Fragility*: "Racism has been among the most complex social dilemmas since the founding of the country. While there is no biological race as we understand it, race as a social construct has profound significance and shapes every aspect of our lives. Race will influence whether we survive at birth, where we are most likely to live, which schools we will attend, who our friends and partners will be, what careers we will have, how much money we will earn, how healthy we will be, and even how long we can expect to live."[120] Every time I reread *White Fragility*, I gain new understandings. See the endnotes for a link to DiAngelo in a lecture that is also worth viewing more than once.[121]

Black Reconstruction in America: 1860-1880, by W. E. B. Du Bois.

Most of the historical accounts of Reconstruction have been written from a white Southern perspective. This account, published in 1935 by America's first Black sociologist and Harvard graduate, was an ambitious attempt to set the record straight. As I have stated earlier, anyone unfamiliar with this period in American history cannot fully appreciate the subject of racial prejudice in this country. This book should be used whenever post-Civil War history is taught. For many years after 1877, life for African Americans in the South was made worse than slavery by the terror tactics of white supremacists. Memories of many of these events are still alive in the South to this day.

Biased: Uncovering the Hidden Prejudice That Shapes What We See, Think, and Do, by Jennifer L. Eberhardt.

Stanford University psychology professor Jennifer L. Eberhardt is a law enforcement consultant and the results of her research in how racial bias plays out in the treatment of minorities deserves intensive public attention. See the endnotes for a link to Eberhardt discussing her work on YouTube.[122]

Why We Snap: Understanding the Rage Circuit in Your Brain, by R. Douglas Fields.

This is a terrific book, especially for peace officers, because it delves into all the types of triggers there are for causing rage. Some of these are guaranteed to happen to law enforcement officers by nature of their duties. Fields lists the threats, the triggers, and how to be ready for them. He calls attention to the kind of training that can help a person keep calm under intense stress and avoid freezing because of the extreme fear in a fight or flight situation. Fields outlines the neural circuitries of threat responses and how our brains at an early age stereotype for the purpose of understanding our life experience. It is hard to find books that focus so much on the type of threats peace officers face that can easily trigger losing control of one's temper. This is an occupational hazard that ends lots of careers.

Blue Bias: An Ex-Cop Turned Philosopher Examines the Learning and Resolve Necessary to End Hidden Prejudice in Policing, by Charles D. Hayes.

My objective in writing *Blue Bias* is to help police officers prevent burnout, reduce the incidents of excessive force, adopt a perspective that prevents cynicism, and increase mutual respect between officers and citizens. *Blue Bias* offers the key subjects to consider when trying to come up with a perspective that will enable police officers to dissipate the inevitable angst that comes from witnessing so much aberrant and immoral behavior that comes with the job in any major city. *Blue Bias* is the kind of book I wish I could have read before giving up on a career in law enforcement only to come to regret having done so. I discuss the history of policing, my experience as a Dallas police officer, and my involvement in the double standard of policing in impoverished neighborhoods that occurred in the 1960s and is still rampant today. I also show how the ethos of learning more about how human behavior as it applies to policing can become a reward in its own right that is as powerful as the adrenaline surges that comes with excitement on the job. I firmly believe that if enough police officers were to adopt the attitude that *Blue Bias* presents, that talk of police reform would not be necessary.

Misogyny: The World's Oldest Prejudice, by Jack Holland.

This book is profoundly important. Jack Holland passed away before *Misogyny* was published and his daughter submitted it for publication. There are lots of books about misogyny, but none that I have found close to this one. Holland puts this subject in crystal-clear perspective, and until you read it, it is difficult to appreciate how much our culture suffers from not fully understanding the persistence of abject misogyny.

The Broken Heart of America: St. Louis and the Violent History of the United States, by Walter Johnson.

Historian Walter Johnson presents a sweeping historical review of racism and imperialism in St. Louis, Missouri, from the expedition of Lewis and Clark to the 2014 uprising in Ferguson. This is a blistering and unforgettable account of exploitation and resistance.

The 1619 Project, edited by Nikole Hannah Jones, Catlin Roper, Ilena Silverman, and Jake Silverstein.

This book by the *New York Times Magazine* is made up of essays, poetry, and fiction pieces by scholars speaking to the very moment we find ourselves in regarding race in America. The chapters titled "Democracy," "Fear," "Dispossession," "Punishment," "Progress," and "Justice" should be required reading in high school.

Race on the Brain: What Implicit Bias Gets Wrong About the Struggle for Racial Justice, by Jonathan Kahn.

A candid and thoughtful examination of the subject of implicit bias and the difficulties of coming to terms with strategies that work. Well-argued and well worth reading and rereading.

Thinking, Fast and Slow, by Daniel Kahneman; and *Noise: A Flaw in Human Judgement*, by Daniel Kahneman, Oliver Sibony, and Cass R. Sunstein.

The most amazing thing about these incredibly insightful books is why it took so long to reach the conclusions that we have two standard modes of thinking—one that's intuitive and one that's more thoughtful. In hindsight, nothing is more obvious, which shows how blind we can be to the things we have always taken for granted. Daniel Kahneman won a Nobel Prize in Economics for his work in challenging rational models of judgment. The insights of these two systems about the way we think are exceptionally relevant to how our minds process bias. *Noise* is an attempt to identify the reasons our thinking often misfires for contextual reasons. This is a hard concept to simplify but it is a very important subject. Reviewers on Amazon complain about it being difficult to nail down, but that is the point. It is exceptionally important that this concept be studied and well understood in law enforcement.

Stamped from the Beginning: The Definitive History of Racist Ideas in America, and *How to Be an Antiracist*, by Ibram X. Kendi.

From the book: "*Stamped from the Beginning* chronicles not just the development of racist ideas, but the ongoing failure of the three oldest and most popular strategies Americans have used to root out these ideas: self-sacrifice, uplift suasion, and educational persuasion."[123] Professor Kendi does that from the days of Cotton Mather through the years of Carter, Reagan, Clinton, Bush, and Obama. *How to Be an Antiracist* is a follow-through with his personal transformation and ideas about systemic racism.

Why We're Polarized, by Ezra Klein.

This is an excellent treatise on today's political polarization. Klein has a chapter titled "Your Brain on Groups" that is very insightful.

The Anatomy of Racial Inequality, by Glenn C. Loury.

This is an exceptionally well-argued treatise on the nature of racial inequality. This book is based on a series of lectures from Professor Loury's W. E. B. DuBois Lectures delivered at Harvard University in April 2000.

Democracy in Chains: The Deep History of the Radical Right's Stealth Plan for America, and *Freedom is Not Enough: The Opening of the American Workplace*,
by Nancy MacLean.

Nancy MacLean is a gifted writer and historian. These works represent her meticulous research in uncovering the threat of ideological authoritarianism in America. *The Atlantic* describes *Democracy in Chains* as "A vibrant intellectual history of the radical right." *Freedom is Not Enough* recalls the recent shameful history of workplace discrimination that has been glossed over and largely forgotten, but is precisely pertinent to today's racial economic inequality.

How the South Won the Civil War: Oligarchy, Democracy, and the Continuing Fight for the Soul of America,
by Heather Cox Richardson.

Characterized as a revisionist history professor, Richardson shows how the authoritarian ideology that gave us the Civil War took a turn to the West when the war was over and was expressed through cowboy culture. A snippet: "Over the course of a generation, both elite slave owners and Movement Conservative leaders came to believe that they alone knew how to run the country."[124] Does this have a familiar ring today?

Everyday Bias: Identifying and Navigating Unconscious Judgements in Our Daily Lives, by Howard Ross.

Hands down, one of the best books in print about bias. In *Blue Bias*, my comments were to implore the reader to read this book and I repeat the recommendation here. See the endnotes for a link to Ross talking about the subject on YouTube.[125]

Behave: The Biology of Humans at Our Best and Worst,
by Robert M. Sapolsky.

This is the best overview of human biology that I have found in print. It is well worth multiple readings. I keep it handy as a reference. It takes a while to let the many areas of this work sink in, and this book brings the point home that human behavior is profoundly complex. Professor Sapolsky has a slew of lectures on YouTube that are well worth your time.[126]

Robert E. Lee and Me: A Southerner's Reckoning with the Myth of the Lost Cause, by Ty Seidule.

This is an examination of Post-Civil War history in the South. It is a passionate, searing, and compelling argument that successfully deconstructs the mythology about Robert. E. Lee and the implied nobility of the Confederacy and The Lost Cause.

How the Word is Passed: A Reckoning with the History of Slavery Across America, by Clint Smith.

Clint Smith tours places in America steeped in the legacy of slavery—former plantations, Confederate Army cemeteries, prisons, and historical sites—taking official tours as he peels away what is commonly understood these places stand for and reveals historical realties far beyond common knowledge. Reading this text, it is stunning how little most people know about history and his interviews with Southerners show how the ideology of the Confederacy still lingers as being, if not the truth, at least based in truth.

A Passion for Justice: Emotions and the Origins of the Social Contract, by Robert C. Solomon.

Professor Solomon passed away in 2007. This is a beautifully written and passionately argued treatise, stating that without individuals whose caring is genuine, the quest for justice is unrealistic and meaningless. This is a great read for psychologically weary police officers and teachers who need to recharge their emotional batteries, so to speak.

To Protect and Serve: How to Fix America's Police, and Breaking Rank: A Top Cop's Expose of the Dark Side of Policing, by Norm Stamper.

Both works offer clear examples of what must be done to reform policing in America. Norm Stamper's candid and upfront observations are rare, but urgently needed.

***The Hidden Brain: How Our Unconscious Minds Elect
Presidents, Control Markets, Wage Wars, and Save Our
Lives***, by Shankar Vedantam.

Shankar Vedantam is a national treasure. *The Hidden Brain*
is full of the insightful ways our lives are influenced and in
fact dominated by our subconscious. Vedantam reminds us
that, "The hidden brain is insidious not because it whacks us
on the back of the head but because it places the tiniest of
fingers on our inner scales."[127] Shankar Vedantam's *Hidden
Brain Podcast* features scores of lectures on subjects related to
biases. See the endnotes for a link to Vedantam discussing *The
Hidden Brain* on YouTube.[128]

ENDNOTES

1. Gordon W. Allport, *The Nature of Prejudice* (New York: Addison Wesley Publishing, 1954, 1979), 328.

2. Jonathan Kahn, *Race on the Brain: What Implicit Bias Gets Wrong About the Struggle for Racial Justice* (New York: Columbia University Press, 2018), 207–223.

3. Kahn, *Race on the Brain*, viii.

4. Kahn, *Race on the Brain*, 67.

5. Kahn, *Race on the Brain*, 225.

6. Kahn, *Race on the Brain*, 216.

7. Kahn, *Race on the Brain*, 226.

8. Kahn, *Race on the Brain*, 227.

9. Kahn, *Race on the Brain*, 227.

10. Allport, *The Nature of Prejudice*, 397.

11. Harry S. Truman, "Truman Quotes," *Truman Library Institute,* 2021, https://www.trumanlibraryinstitute.org/truman/truman-quotes/.

12. Liam Stack, "Over 1,000 Hate Groups Are Now Active in United States, Civil Rights Group Says," *The New York Times,* February 20, 2019, https://www.nytimes.com/2019/02/20/us/hate-groups-rise.html.

13. Berit Brogaard, *Hatred: Understanding Our Most Dangerous Emotion* (New York: Oxford University Press, 2020), 259.

14. Robert M. Sapolsky, *Behave: The Biology of Humans at Our Best and Worst* (New York: Penguin Press, 2017), 453.

15. Richard Delgado and Jean Stefancic, *Critical Race Theory: An Introduction* (New York: New York University Press, 2017), 1–15.

16. Vivek Ramaswamy, *Woke, Inc: Inside Corporate America's Social Justice Scam* (New York: Center Street, 2021), 30.

17. Ramaswamy, *Woke, Inc.,* 44.

18. Ramaswamy, *Woke, Inc.,* 240–259.

19. Ramaswamy, *Woke, Inc.,* 5, 133, 216, 227, 262, 266–267, 269, 325.

20. Kahn, *Race on the Brain*, 110.

21. Steven Pinker, *Rationality: What It Is, Why It Seems Scarce, Why It Matters* (New York: Viking, 2021), 123.

22. David W. Blight, *Race and Reunion: The Civil War in American Memory* (Cambridge, MA: The Belknap Press, 2001), 101–105, 109–111, 112–114.

23. Charles Murray and Richard J. Herrnstein, *The Bell Curve: Intelligence and Class Structure in American Life* (New York: The Free Press, 1996).

24. W. E. B. Du Bois, *Black Reconstruction in America: 1860-1880* (New York: The Free Press, 1962, 1965), 670.

25. Du Bois, *Black Reconstruction*, 726.

26. Douglas A. Blackmon, *Slavery by Another Name: The Re-Enslavement of Black Americans from the Civil War to World War II* (New York: Doubleday, 2008), 6–8.

27. W. Fitzhugh Brundage, *Lynching in the New South: Georgia and Virginia, 1880-1930* (Chicago, IL: University of Illinois Press, 1993), 1.

28. Brundage, *Lynching in the New South*, 6.

29. Brundage, *Lynching in the New South*, 8.

30. Brundage, *Lynching in the New South*, 25.

31. Brundage, *Lynching in the New South*, 57.

32. Murray and Herrnstein, *The Bell Curve*.

33. John McWhorter, *Woke Racism: How a New Religion Has Betrayed Black America* (New York: Penguin, 2021).

34. John McWhorter, "Racism in American Is Over," *Forbes*, December 30, 2008, https://www.forbes.com/2008/12/30/end-of-racism-oped-cx_jm_1230mcwhorter.html.

35. Heather Cox Richardson, *How the South Won the Civil War: Oligarchy, Democracy, and the Continuing Fight for the Soul of America* (New York: Oxford University Press, 2020), xiv.

36. Kristin Kobes Du Mez, *Jesus and John Wayne: How White Evangelicals Corrupted a Faith and Fractured a Nation* (New York: Liveright Publishing Corporation, 2020), 37.

37. Ty Seidule, *Robert E. Lee and Me: A Southerner's Reckoning with the Myth of the Lost Cause* (New York: St Martin's Press, 2020), 30.

38. Seidule, *Robert E. Lee and Me*, 42–57.

39. Blight, *Race and Reunion*, 258.

40. Charles Reagan Wilson, *Baptized in Blood: The Religion of the Lost Cause: 1865-1920* (Athens, GA: The University of Georgia Press, 1980, 2009).

41. Seidule, *Robert E. Lee and Me*, 39–41.

42. Nancy MacLean, *Democracy in Chains: The Deep History of the Radical Right's Stealth Plan for America* (New York: Penguin, 2017), xiii, xv, xviii–xix, 12, 13–20, 46, 48–52, 74, 133, 208, 217, 229.

43. Sapolsky, *Behave*, 430.

44. Sapolsky, *Behave*, 391, 392.

45. Sapolsky, *Behave*, 442.

46. Sapolsky, *Behave*, 116–117, 135, 389, 614.

47. Sapolsky, *Behave*, 116–117.

48. Sapolsky, *Behave*, 135.

49. Suzanne Daley, "Nordic Countries, Overwhelmed by Migrants, Retreat from Generous Traditions," *The New York Times*, November 16, 2011, https://www.nytimes.com/2015/11/16/world/europe/nordic-countries-overwhelmed-by-migrants-retreat-from-generous-traditions.html.

50. Sapolsky, *Behave*, 25, 38, 42–43, 59, 88.

51. Sapolsky, *Behave*, 34.

52. Glenn C. Loury, *The Anatomy of Racial Inequality* (Cambridge, MA: Harvard University Press, 2021), 24.

53. Gerhard Falk, *Stigma: How We Treat Outsiders* (New York: Prometheus Books, 2001), 11.

54. Isabel Wilkerson, *Caste: The Origins of Our Discontents* (New York: Random House, 2020), 289–290.

55. Paul Bloom, *Just Babies: The Origins of Good and Evil* (New York: Crown Publishers, 2013), 14.

56. Ezra Klein, *Why We're Polarized* (New York: Avid Reader Press, 2020), 57.

57. Shankar Vedantam, *The Hidden Brain: How Our Unconscious Minds Elect Presidents, Control Markets, Wage Wars, and Save Our Lives* (New York: Spiegel & Grau, 2010), 22.

58. R. Douglas Fields, *Why We Snap: Understanding the Rage Circuit in Your Brain* (New York: Dutton, 2015), 307.

59. Fields, *Why We Snap*, 308.

60. Allport, *The Nature of Prejudice*, 8.

61. Vedantam, *The Hidden Brain*, 72–73.

62. David Berreby, *Us and Them: The Science of Identity* (Chicago, IL: University of Chicago Press, 2008), xiii, 93–116.

63. Sapolsky, *Behave*, 85.

64. Sapolsky, *Behave*, 391–392.

65. John Tooby, "Coalitional Instincts," *Edge*, November 22, 2017, https://www. edge.org/conversation/john_tooby-coalitional-instincts.

66. Daniel Kahneman, *Thinking, Fast and Slow* (New York: Random House, 2011), 27–28, 64–65, 81.

67. Kahneman, *Thinking, Fast and Slow*, 387.

68. Daniel Kahneman, Oliver Sibony, and Cass R. Sunstein, *Noise: A Flaw in Human Judgment* (New York: Little Brown Spark, 2021), 6–10.

69. Kahneman, Sibony, and Sunstein, *Noise*, 17.

70. Kahneman, Sibony, and Sunstein, *Noise*, 173.

71. Michelle Alexander, *The New Jim Crow: Mass Incarceration in the Age of Colorblindness* (New York: The New Press, 2010), 2.

72. Alexander, *The New Jim Crow*, 228.

73. Alexander, *The New Jim Crow*, 228–229.

74. Jim McCambridge, John Witton, and Diana B. Elbourne, "Systematic Review of the Hawthorne Effect: New Concepts Are Needed to Study Research Participation Effects," *Journal of Clinical Epidemiology* 67(3): 267–277 (March 2014), https://www.ncbi.nlm.nih.gov/pmc/articles/ PMC3969247/.

75. James Baldwin, "Unnamable Objects and Unspeakable Crimes," in *The White Problem in America* (Chicago: Johnson Publishing, 1966), 173–181.

76. Kehinde Andrews, *The New Age of Empire: How Racism and Colonialism Still Rule the World* (New York: Bold Type Books, 2021), 2–19. Andrews makes note of the racist attitudes of John Locke, David Hume, Immanuel Kant, Voltaire, and Georg Wilhelm Friedrich Hegel.

77. Walter Johnson, *The Broken Heart of America: St. Louis and the Violent History of the United States* (New York: Basic Books, 2020), 363.

78. United States Department of Justice: Civil Rights Division, "Investigation of the Ferguson Police Department," The United States Department of Justice, March 4, 2015, https://www.justice.gov/sites/default/files/opa/press-releases/ attachments/2015/03/04/ferguson_police_department_report.pdf.

79. United States Department of Justice, "Investigation of the Ferguson Police Department," https://www.justice.gov/sites/default/files/opa/press-releases/ attachments/2015/03/04/ferguson_police_department_report.pdf.

80. Sapolsky, *Behave*, 88.

81. Fields, *Why We Snap*, 308, 309.

82. Ibram X. Kendi, *How To Be An Antiracist* (New York: One World, 2019), 48.

83. Jennifer L. Eberhardt, *Biased: Uncovering the Hidden Prejudice that Shapes What We See, Think, and Do* (New York: Viking, 2019), 103, 104, 105.

84. Charles D. Hayes, *Blue Bias: An Ex-Cop Turned Philosopher Examines the Learning and Resolve Necessary to End Hidden Prejudice in Policing* (Wasilla, AK: Autodidactic Press, 2020), 43–58.

85. Ta-Nehisi Coates, "The Case for Reparations," *The Atlantic*, June 2014, https://www.theatlantic.com/magazine/archive/2014/06/the-case-for-reparations/361631/.

86. David Eagleman, *Livewired: The Inside Story of the Ever-Changing Brain* (New York: Penguin Random House, 2020), 11.

87. Kahneman, Sibony, and Sunstein, *Noise*, 250–253.

88. Loury, *The Anatomy of Racial Inequality*, 167.

89. Nancy MacLean, *Freedom is Not Enough: The Opening of the American Workplace* (New York: The Russell Sage Foundation, 2006), 1–10.

90. MacLean, *Freedom is Not Enough*, 1–3.

91. Sheryll Cashin, *White Space, Black Hood: Opportunity Hoarding and Segregation in the Age of Inequality* (Boston, MA: Beacon Press, 2021), 4.

92. Cashin, *White Space, Black Hood*, 6.

93. Nikole Hannah Jones, Catlin Roper, Ilena Silverman, and Jake Silverstein, eds., *The 1619 Project* (New York: One World, 2021), 436.

94. Loury, *The Anatomy of Racial Inequality*, xxiv.

95. Hayes, *Blue Bias*, 288.

96. Sapolsky, *Behave*, 46, 59, 516–19, 528–34, 547, 559–60, 622.

97. Charlie May, "FBI investigated white supremacists infiltrating law enforcement agencies: A report," Salon.com, January 31, 2017, https://www.salon.com/2017/01/31/fbi-investigating-white-supremacists-infiltrating-law-enforcement-agencies-report/.

98. Sapolsky, *Behave*, 107–17, 133, 134, 135, 530.

99. Tony Greenwald, Mahzarin Banaji, and Brian Nosek, "Project Implicit," Harvard University, 2011, https://implicit.harvard.edu/implicit/takeatest.html.

100. Kahn, *Race on the Brain*, 216–220.

101. Mark Edmundson, *Why Teach: In Defense of Real Education* (New York: Bloomsbury, 2013), 59. Here is Mark Edmundson on *Why Teach*: Elmhurst University, "Mark Edmundson: Why Teach? In Defense of a Real Education," YouTube Video, 1:05:38, May 19, 2014, https://www.youtube.com/watch?v=LtKnCbGt3bM.

102. William James, *Talks to Teachers On Psychology and to Students on Some of Life's Ideals* (New York: Henry Holt, 1899, 1962), 17.

103. Neil Postman, *Conscientious Objections: Stirring Up Trouble about Language, Technology, and Education* (New York: Alfred A. Knopf, Inc., 1988), 22.

104. Neil Postman, *Technopoly: The Surrender of Culture to Technology* (New York: Alfred A. Knopf, 1992), 174.

105. Postman, *Conscientious Objections,* 21.

106. Postman, *Conscientious Objections,* 26.

107. Todd Rose, *Collective Illusions: Conformity, Complicity and the Science of Why We Make Bad Decisions* (New York: Hachette Books, 2022), 118. I love the term "corrupted norm." Rose writes, "Entire societies can participate in destructive behaviors that people don't actually condone, such as racism, sexism, and other forms of bigotry. And because we're not aware of how this happens, corrupted norms lurk under the rocks, like rattlesnakes."

108. David Graeber and David Wengrow, *The Dawn of Everything: A New History of Humanity* (New York: Farrar, Straus and Giroux, 2021).

109. Norman Cotterell and Dara Friedman-Wheeler, "CBT and Anti-Racism: Healing Racism Through CBT," *CBT Insights,* June 8, 2021, Beck Institute, https://beckinstitute.org/blog/cbt-and-anti-racism-healing-racism-through-cbt/.

110. Graeber and Wengrow, *The Dawn of Everything,* 174.

111. Sigmund Freud, "Freud," in *Great Books of the Western World, Volume 54* (Chicago: Encyclopaedia Britannica, Inc., 1952), 788.

112. Rose, *Collective Illusions,* 103.

113. Leonard Mlodinow, *Emotional: How Feelings Shape Our Thinking* (New York: Pantheon Books, 2022), xv, 56–57.

114. Fields, *Why We Snap,* 310. Citing the work of psychologist David Amodio of New York University, Fields reports that these implicit biases, because they were acquired unconsciously, are very difficult to change.

115. Ursula Bellugi and Marie St. George, Eds., *Journey from Cognition to Brain to Gene: Perspectives from Williams Syndrome* (Cambridge, MA: The MIT Press, 2001).

116. Alexander, *The New Jim Crow,* 6.

117. NYU School of Law, " 'The New Jim Crow' Author Michelle Alexander on Derrick Bell's Legacy," YouTube Video, 1:17:56, November 8, 2016, https://www.youtube.com/watch?v=znQ3CR---Kw.

118. Berreby, *Us and Them,* 31.

119. Bloggingheads.tv, "Science Saturday: Tribes and Prejudices | John Horgan & David Berreby [Science Saturday]," YouTube Video, 1:11:33, April 5, 2018, https://www.youtube.com/watch?v=6TlEC64XRa4.

120. Robin DiAngelo, *White Fragility: Why It's So Hard for White People to Talk About Racism* (Boston, MA: Beacon Press, 2018), 5.

121. Seattle Channel, "Dr. Robin DiAngelo discusses 'White Fragility,' " YouTube Video, 1:23:30, July 3, 2018, https://www.youtube.com/watch?v=45ey4jgoxeU.

122. Politics and Prose, "Jennifer L. Eberhardt, 'Biased,' " YouTube Video, 1:10:43, November 24, 2019, https://www.youtube.com/watch?v=YudEO_jRWww.

123. Ibram X. Kendi, *Stamped from the Beginning: The Definitive History of Racist Ideas* (New York: Nation Books, 2016), 503.

124. Richardson, *How the South Won the Civil War*, xiv.

125. Franklin Covey, "Bias Isn't Always Bad | Howard Ross Clip," YouTube Video, 1:47, September 5, 2019, https://www.youtube.com/watch?v=e2MpEut89HA.

126. Fred Flintstone, " 'Behave' by Robert Sapolsky, PhD," YouTube Video, 57:15, July 18, 2017, https://www.youtube.com/watch?v=k5rUwupQSQY.

127. Vedantam, *The Hidden Brain*, 79.

128. GBH Forum Network, "Shankar Vedantam: The Hidden Brain," YouTube Video, 57:17, November 29, 2012, https://www.youtube.com/watch?v=a5aB2RkPkro.

BIBLIOGRAPHY

Alexander, Michelle. *The New Jim Crow: Mass Incarceration in the Age of Colorblindness* (New York: The New Press, 2010).

Allport, Gordon W. *The Nature of Prejudice* (New York: Addison Wesley Publishing, 1954, 1979).

Andrews, Kehinde. *The New Age of Empire: How Racism and Colonialism Still Rule the World* (New York: Bold Type Books, 2021).

Baldwin, James. "Unnamable Objects and Unspeakable Crimes," in James Baldwin, *The White Problem in America* (Chicago: Johnson Publishing, 1966).

Bellugi, Ursula, and Marie St. George, Eds. *Journey from Cognition to Brain to Gene: Perspectives from Williams Syndrome* (Cambridge, MA: The MIT Press, 2001).

Berreby, David. *Us and Them: The Science of Identity* (Chicago, IL: University of Chicago Press, 2008).

Blackmon, Douglas A. *Slavery by Another Name: The Re-Enslavement of Black Americans from the Civil War to World War II* (New York: Doubleday, 2008).

Blight, David W. *Race and Reunion: The Civil War in American Memory* (Cambridge, MA: The Belknap Press, 2001).

Bloom, Paul. *Just Babies: The Origins of Good and Evil* (New York: Crown Publishers, 2013).

Brogaard, Berit. *Hatred: Understanding Our Most Dangerous Emotion* (New York: Oxford University Press, 2020).

Brundage, W. Fitzhugh. *Lynching in the New South: Georgia and Virginia, 1880-1930* (Chicago, IL: University of Illinois Press, 1993).

Cashin, Sheryll. *White Space, Black Hood: Opportunity Hoarding and Segregation in the Age of Inequality* (Boston, MA: Beacon Press, 2021).

Coates, Ta-Nehisi. "The Case for Reparations." *The Atlantic*, June 2014. https://www.theatlantic.com/magazine/archive/2014/06/the-case-for-reparations/361631/.

127

Cotterell, Norman, and Dara Friedman-Wheeler. "CBT and Anti-Racism: Healing Racism Through CBT." *CBT Insights*, June 8, 2021. Beck Institute. https://beckinstitute.org/blog/cbt-and-anti-racism-healing-racism-through-cbt/.

Daley, Suzanne. "Nordic Countries, Overwhelmed by Migrants, Retreat from Generous Traditions." *The New York Times*, November 16, 2011. https://www.nytimes.com/2015/11/16/world/europe/nordic-countries-overwhelmed-by-migrants-retreat-from-generous-traditions.html.

Delgado, Richard, and Jean Stefancic. *Critical Race Theory: An Introduction* (New York: New York University Press, 2017).

DiAngelo, Robin. *White Fragility: Why It's So Hard for White People to Talk About Racism* (Boston, MA: Beacon Press, 2018).

Du Bois, W. E. B. *Black Reconstruction in America: 1860-1880* (New York: The Free Press, 1962, 1965).

Du Mez, Kristin Kobes. *Jesus and John Wayne: How White Evangelicals Corrupted a Faith and Fractured a Nation.* (New York: Liverright Publishing Corporation, 2020).

Eagleman, David. *Livewired: The Inside Story of the Ever-Changing Brain* (New York: Penguin Random House, 2020).

Eberhardt, Jennifer L. *Biased: Uncovering the Hidden Prejudice that Shapes What We See, Think, and Do* (New York: Viking, 2019).

Edmundson, Mark. *Why Teach: In Defense of Real Education* (New York: Bloomsbury, 2013).

Falk, Gerhard. *Stigma: How We Treat Outsiders* (New York: Prometheus Books, 2001).

Fields, R. Douglas. *Why We Snap: Understanding the Rage Circuit in Your Brain* (New York: Dutton, 2015).

Freud, Sigmund. "Freud." In *Great Books of the Western World, Volume 54* (Chicago: Encyclopaedia Britannica, Inc., 1952).

Graeber, David, and David Wengrow. *The Dawn of Everything: A New History of Humanity* (New York: Farrar, Straus and Giroux, 2021).

Greenwald, Tony, Mahzarin Banaji, and Brian Nosek. "Project Implicit." Harvard University, 2011. https://implicit.harvard.edu/implicit/takeatest.html.

Hayes, Charles D. *Blue Bias: An Ex-Cop Turned Philosopher Examines the Learning and Resolve Necessary to End Hidden Prejudice in Policing* (Wasilla, AK: Autodidactic Press, 2020).

James, William. *Talks to Teachers On Psychology and to Students on Some of Life's Ideals* (New York: Henry Holt, 1899, 1962).

Johnson, Walter. *The Broken Heart of America: St. Louis and the Violent History of the United States* (New York: Basic Books, 2020).

Jones, Nikole Hannah, Catlin Roper, Ilena Silverman, and Jake Silverstein, Eds. *The 1619 Project* (New York: One World, 2021).

Kahn, Jonathan. *Race on the Brain: What Implicit Bias Gets Wrong About the Struggle for Racial Justice* (New York: Columbia University Press, 2018).

Kahneman, Daniel. *Thinking, Fast and Slow* (New York: Random House, 2011).

Kahneman, Daniel, Oliver Sibony, and Cass R. Sunstein. *Noise: A Flaw in Human Judgment,* (New York: Little Brown Spark, 2021).

Kendi, Ibram X. *Stamped from the Beginning: The Definitive History of Racist Ideas* (New York: Nation Books, 2016).

—. *How To Be An Antiracist* (New York: One World, 2019).

Klein, Ezra. *Why We're Polarized* (New York: Avid Reader Press, 2020).

Loury, Glenn C. *The Anatomy of Racial Inequality* (Cambridge, MA: Harvard University Press, 2021).

MacLean, Nancy. *Freedom is Not Enough: The Opening of the American Workplace* (New York: The Russell Sage Foundation, 2006).

—. *Democracy in Chains: The Deep History of the Radical Right's Stealth Plan for America* (New York: Penguin, 2017).

May, Charlie. "FBI investigated white supremacists infiltrating law enforcement agencies: A report." Salon.com, January 31, 2017. https://www.salon.com/2017/01/31/fbi-investigating-white-supremacists-infiltrating-law-enforcement-agencies-report/.

McCambridge, Jim, John Witton, and Diana B. Elbourne. "Systematic Review of the Hawthorne Effect: New Concepts Are Needed to Study Research Participation Effects." *Journal of Clinical Epidemiology* 67(3): 267–277 (March 2014). https://www.ncbi.nlm.nih.gov/pmc/articles/PMC3969247/.

McWhorter, John. "Racism in American Is Over." *Forbes,* December 30, 2008. https://www.forbes.com/2008/12/30/end-of-racism-oped-cx_jm_1230mcwhorter.html.

—. *Woke Racism: How a New Religion Has Betrayed Black America* (New York: Penguin, 2021).

Mlodinow, Leonard. *Emotional: How Feelings Shape Our Thinking* (New York: Pantheon Books, 2022).

Murray, Charles, and Richard J. Herrnstein. *The Bell Curve: Intelligence and Class Structure in American Life* (New York: The Free Press, 1996).

Postman, Neil. *Conscientious Objections: Stirring Up Trouble about Language, Technology, and Education* (New York: Alfred A. Knopf, Inc., 1988).

—. *Technopoly: The Surrender of Culture to Technology* (New York: Alfred A. Knopf, 1992).

Pinker, Steven. *Rationality: What It Is, Why It Seems Scarce, Why It Matters* (New York: Viking, 2021).

Ramaswamy, Vivek. *Woke, Inc: Inside Corporate America's Social Justice Scam* (New York: Center Street, 2021).

Richardson, Heather Cox. *How the South Won the Civil War: Oligarchy, Democracy, and the Continuing Fight for the Soul of America* (New York: Oxford University Press, 2020).

Rose, Todd. *Collective Illusions: Conformity, Complicity, and the Science of Why We Make Bad Decisions* (New York: Hachette Books, 2022).

Sapolsky, Robert M. *Behave: The Biology of Humans at Our Best and Worst* (New York: Penguin Press, 2017).

Seidule, Ty. *Robert E. Lee and Me: A Southerner's Reckoning with the Myth of the Lost Cause* (New York: St Martin's Press, 2020).

Stack, Liam. "Over 1,000 Hate Groups Are Now Active in United States, Civil Rights Group Says." *The New York Times*, February 20, 2019. https://www.nytimes.com/2019/02/20/us/hate-groups-rise.html.

Tooby, John. "Coalitional Instincts." *Edge*, November 22, 2017. https://www.edge.org/conversation/john_tooby-coalitional-instincts.

Truman, Harry S. "Truman Quotes." *Truman Library Institute,* 2021. https://www.trumanlibraryinstitute.org/truman/truman-quotes/.

United States Department of Justice: Civil Rights Division. "Investigation of the Ferguson Police Department." The United States Department of Justice, March 4, 2015. https://www.justice.gov/sites/default/files/opa/press-releases/attachments/2015/03/04/ferguson_police_department_report.pdf.

Vedantam, Shankar. *The Hidden Brain: How Our Unconscious Minds Elect Presidents, Control Markets, Wage Wars, and Save Our Lives* (New York: Spiegel & Grau, 2010).

Wilkerson, Isabel. *Caste: The Origins of Our Discontents* (New York: Random House, 2020).

Wilson, Charles Reagan. *Baptized in Blood: The Religion of the Lost Cause: 1865-1920* (Athens, GA: The University of Georgia Press, 1980, 2009).

INDEX

ABOUT THE AUTHOR

CHARLES D. HAYES is a self-taught philosopher and one of America's strongest advocates for lifelong learning. He spent his youth in Texas and served as a U.S. Marine and as a police officer before embarking on a career in the oil industry. Alaska has been his home for more than forty years.

Promoting the idea that education should be thought of not as something you get but as something you take, Hayes' work has been featured in *The L.A. Progressive*, *USA Today*, and the *UTNE Reader*, on National Public Radio's *Talk of the Nation* and on Alaska Public Radio's *Talk of Alaska*.

Praised for his remarkable depth of knowledge across numerous disciplines, Hayes affirms through his work that active, continuous learning is what makes life worthwhile. His books encourage the kind of thinking that can transform human relations on a global scale, urging us to continuously examine our values, motivations, and common beliefs. He inspires us to acknowledge our mortality and live authentically as a result, taking deliberate action to leave the world a better place than we found it.

"The temporary nature of our lives may be a reason for unavoidable despair," says Hayes, "but such is the price of intelligence—it doesn't render our lives meaningless. To the contrary, the opportunity to live a life as a human being makes us the most fortunate creatures on the planet. We should be experts at being human and creating a world where humans can thrive."

Also by Charles D. Hayes

Fiction

The Call of Mortality

Portals in a Northern Sky

Pansy: Bovine Genius in Wild Alaska

Stalking Cindy

Moose Hunter Homicide

A Mile North of Good and Evil

Benzeerilla

Nonfiction

Blue Bias: An Ex-Cop Turned Philosopher Examines the Learning and Resolve Necessary to End Hidden Prejudice in Policing

September University: Summoning Passion for an Unfinished Life

Existential Aspirations: Reflections of a Self-Taught Philosopher

In Defense of Liberal Ideas

The Rapture of Maturity: A Legacy of Lifelong Learning

Training Yourself: The 21st Century Credential

Beyond the American Dream: Lifelong Learning and the Search for Meaning in a Postmodern World

Proving You're Qualified: Strategies for Competent People without College Degrees

Self-University: The Price of Tuition Is the Desire to Learn. Your Degree Is a Better Life

What Others Say About the Work of Charles D. Hayes

"In a world of flabby, fragmentary, and postmodernist thinking, Hayes offers a glowing tribute to old-fashioned curiosity and reason. Clear thinking is as human and healthy as breathing. Charles Hayes encourages us to give it a try."

—BARBARA EHRENREICH, author of *Fear of Falling* and *Blood Rites*

"In the midst of all the frantic hype and fluff that deluge Americans every day and produce so much ovine behavior, it is an inspiration to hear from someone who both cherishes and exemplifies independent thinking."

—PHILIP SLATER, author of *The Pursuit of Loneliness* and *A Dream Deferred*

"Reading *Portals* is like looking through a kaleidoscope in which breakneck adventure and science fiction occasionally reconfigure themselves into patterns of ancient wisdom—don't start unless you have enough time to finish it, because you won't be able to put it down."

—MIHALY CSIKSZENTMIHALYI, author of *Flow* and *The Evolving Self*

"Charles Hayes' voice is one of experienced wisdom, grappling artfully with the 'existential' questions we all grapple with, well or poorly. His answers, his appreciation of the role of Emersonian ecstasy in education, and his reflections on things that matter, are well worth your consideration."

—ROBERT C. SOLOMON author of *Spirituality for the Skeptic: The Thoughtful Love of Life* and coauthor of *A Passion for Wisdom*

"*The Rapture of Maturity* takes the reader on a wonderful intellectual journey through the author's own lived experiences as well as some timeless scholarly works on the mysteries of human existence. The book is a rich tapestry in which threads of insight are interwoven by the author into a fabric of wisdom, providing the reader with a comforting blanket of understanding regarding some of the more distressing aspects of being human."

—JAMES CÔTÉ, author of *Arrested Adulthood: The Changing Nature of Maturity and Identity*

"I agree with Charles Hayes when he says, 'Nothing is as it seems.' He clearly understands that we must make efforts to overcome our conditioning if we are to fulfill our potential. *The Rapture of Maturity* spells out why it is important for all human beings to be stretched (not stressed) throughout our lives, to always inquire about the truth of things, and to serve others."

—IVAN TYRRELL, coauthor of *Human Givens:*
A New Approach to Emotional Health and Clear Thinking

"*The Rapture of Maturity* is one of those rare books that one only realizes, after it gets written, how desperately needed it was. At a time when self-help books for the 'boomers' are both endemic and anemic, this one is a trumpet blast of authenticity, courage, and useable erudition."

—RONALD GROSS, author of *The Lifelong Learner and Socrates' Way*
and chairman at Columbia University Seminar on Innovation

"*The Rapture of Maturity* is an exquisitely thoughtful book. Hayes has a lovely spirit and strong insights into the springs of personal power."

—JOHN TAYLOR GATTO, former New York Teacher of the Year and author of
The Underground History of American Education

"*September University* is a nourishing feast of a book, replete with reasons to discover new meaning and purpose in the last chapters of your life, to welcome those years as life's most precious gift—an opportunity to cultivate wisdom and then put it to use in the world."

—WALTER TRUETT ANDERSON, President Emeritus at
World Academy of Art and Science

"*September University* is the first philosophy integrating the university without walls and transformative learning—essential reading for learning in the 21st century."

—DANIEL S. JANIK, MD, PhD, author of *Unlock the Genius Within:*
Neurobiological Trauma, Teaching, and Transformative Learning

"*September University* is a wonderful book. It is wise and passionate and can teach us all about the rare art of growing old."

—SAM KEEN, philosopher and author of *Faces of the Enemy*

"It's not too late to make your mark on the world and enjoy a new level of fulfillment in your life. Charles Hayes will inspire you to muster the courage to do it."

—JEFF SCHMIDT, author of *Disciplined Minds*

"*September University*, by leading scholar and visionary Charles Hayes, is a superb intellectual achievement by any standards. With sweeping scope and remarkable depth of knowledge across numerous disciplines, Hayes addresses the totality of the human experience—along with neglected questions surrounding life, death, freedom, authenticity, and truth—as he paves the way for a genuinely mature future in which citizens discover new degrees of potency and thoughtfulness. Rather than shying away from idealism, *September University* sets out a bold and timely blueprint for a post-consumer consciousness that is more culturally aware, media literate, and politically astute. Hayes delves with electrifying intelligence into the nature of meaning, identity, and community as he weaves together a comprehensive philosophy that enables people to transcend evolutionary baggage, social indoctrination, and illusions of limitation. *September University* is one of the finest books in print when it comes to the wisdom and existential bearings required to survive the current age of insanity."

—JOHN F. SCHUMAKER, author of *In Search of Happiness: Understanding an Endangered State of Mind, Wings of Illusion, and The Age of Insanity*

"This is an important work. Wisdom evolves from real-life experience, and Charles Hayes has both. For those who aspire to a better world, this is a must read."

—PETER C. WHYBROW, Director of the Semel Institute for Neuroscience and Human Behavior at UCLA and author of *American Mania: When More Is Not Enough*

"Engaging, convincing, and provocative. Given the collapse of the future most adults thought they had, and the involuntary mandate to shape a new one, *September University* calls those in the second half of life to step away from superficial things and commit to becoming wise guides for the generations that come after them."

—DAVID L. SOLIE, MS, PA, author of *How to Say It to Seniors*

Made in the USA
Middletown, DE
25 April 2023

29122793R00090